50 Crochet Dishcloths

50 Crochet Dishcloths by WeCrochet.
Copyright ©2021, Crafts Group, LLC.

The contents of the publications are the sole property of Crafts Group, LLC and intended for personal use only, except by reviewers who may quote brief passages. For pattern support, please contact customerservice@wecrochet.com.

Photography by Regan Nishikawa and Amy Cave

Book Design by Zoey Stencil

Editorial by Katelyn Moll, Heather Mann, and Sara Dudek

Technical Editing by Tian Connaughton and Kristine Mullen

Printed in the United States of America

First Printing, 2021

ISBN 978-1-62767-309-9

Versa Press, Inc.
800-447-7829
www.versapress.com

With 50 crochet patterns to choose from, this collection has everything you need to make your home shine! *50 Crochet Dishcloths* features patterns both simple and complex to ensure your dishes, hands, and face are always squeaky clean. Learn some new techniques or find some new dishcloth inspiration with these tasteful textiles that are quick makes, perfect for last-minute gifts or for use in your own home.

Contents

- 9   Wavy Chevron
- 11   Little Leaves
- 13   Confused Textures
- 15   Ebb + Flow
- 17   Alpine Stitch
- 19   Ribbon Candy
- 21   Textured Comb
- 23   Misty Rose
- 25   Golden Lattice
- 27   Cookies & Cream
- 29   Glacial Spa
- 31   Mismatched
- 33   Creamsicle
- 35   Orbital
- 37   Dragonfly Delight
- 39   Peach Margot
- 41   Celtic Weave
- 43   Tunisian Purl Stitch
- 45   Nice-n-Easy
- 47   Teal Swirl
- 49   Dancing Shells
- 51   Log Cabin
- 53   Cabled Spa
- 55   Tunisian Lattice
- 57   The Jerrica
- 59   Berry Jam Jar
- 61   Étoile
- 63   Hipacious Houndstooth

65	Mitered Square	81	Diagonal Cloth	97	Custard Pie
67	Jazz Age	83	Picnic Basket	99	A Chance of Rain
69	Rib Texture	85	Snuggle Stitch	101	Chevron
71	Sloped Lines	87	Gingham Twist	103	Sophia Spa
73	Sherbet Tunisian	89	Brick-a-Brack	105	Tunisian Seed Stitch
75	Fruity Loops	91	The Sun's Out!	107	Heirloom Linen
77	Multi Chevron	93	Marguerite		
79	Granny's Rainbow	95	C2C Color Fade		

Wavy Chevron

by Jenny Konopinski | 55545

Striped or solid, the crocheted chevron is a classic pattern that works up quickly and is easy to memorize—the perfect recipe for a satisfying dishcloth. The chevron pattern also builds on the beginning crocheter's skill set with double crochets, increases, and decreases. This pattern includes two sizes.

FINISHED MEASUREMENTS
8.5" (11.5)" square

YARN
Dishie™ (worsted weight, 100% Cotton, 190 yards/100g): MC Lilac Mist 27038, C1 Azure 25412, 1 skein each

HOOKS
US G/6 (4mm) Crochet hook or size needed to obtain gauge

NOTIONS
Yarn Needle
Scissors

GAUGE
10 sts = 2.75" in chevron pattern

Special Stitches

DC3tog (double crochet 3 stitches together)
YO, insert hook into next st, YO and draw up a lp, YO and pull through 2 lps 3 times total. There will be 4 lps on your hook, YO and pull through all lps. 2 sts dec.

Stripe Sequence for small dishcloth
Rows 1-4: Lilac Mist
Rows 5-8: Azure
Rows 9-10: Lilac Mist
Rows 11-12: Azure
Rows 13-16: Lilac Mist

DIRECTIONS
Ch 33 sts.
Row 1: DC into third ch from hook, *DC into next 3 ch each, DC3tog over next 3 ch sts, DC into next 3 ch, 3 DC into next ch* ending the last rep by working 2 DC into last ch instead of 3, turn.
Row 2: Ch 3, DC into first st, *DC into next 3 ch, DC3tog over next 3 sts, DC into next 3, 3 DC into next st* ending the last rep by working 2 DC into Tch, turn.

Rep only Row 2 for 14 (20) more rows or until dishcloth measures 8.5 (11.5)" long.

Finishing
Weave in ends, wash, and block to size.

Little Leaves

by Jenny Konopinski | 55583

Bobbles are a simple way to add texture while adding loads of scrubbing power to your dishcloth! This dishcloth focuses on the bobble stitch to keep things easy and simple, just the thing for a quick weekend project or merely to learn a new stitch.

FINISHED MEASUREMENTS
10" square

YARN
Dishie™ (worsted weight, 100% Cotton, 190 yards/100g): Jalapeño 25785, 1 skein

HOOKS
US F/5 (3.75mm) Crochet hook or size needed to obtain gauge

NOTIONS
Yarn Needle
Scissors

GAUGE
2 bobbles = 1" in pattern

Special Stitches
Bobble (bo)
(YO and insert hook in st, YO and draw lp through st, YO and draw through first 2 lps on hook) 3 times all into the same st, YO and draw lp through all 4 lps on hook to complete the bobble.

DIRECTIONS
Loosely ch 40 sts.
Row 1: Work bo in fourth ch from hook, ch 1, *sk 1, bo in next ch * rep to end, turn.
Row 2: Ch 3, *1 bo in next 1-ch sp between bos of previous row, ch 1* rep to end, working last bo in Tch, turn.

Rep Row 2 until dishcloth measures approximately 10" long.

Finishing
Weave in ends, wash, and block to size.

Confused Textures

by Jennifer Pionk | 56000

If you live for texture, this dishcloth won't disappoint! It looks great in variegated and solids. For a little more punch, add a couple of stripes in a contrasting color.

FINISHED MEASUREMENTS
8.25" wide x 8" high

YARN
Dishie™ Multi (worsted weight, 100% Cotton, 190 yards/100g): Berry Basket 28087, 1 skein

HOOKS
US I/9 (5.5mm) Crochet hook or size needed to obtain gauge
US H/8 (5mm) Crochet hook or size needed to obtain gauge

NOTIONS
Yarn Needle
Scissors

GAUGE
15 sts and 14 rows = 4" in Mini-Bean Stitch

Special Stitches

Mini-Bean Stitch (MBS)
Insert your hook into the st specified, YO, pull up a lp, YO, insert your hook into the same st, YO, pull up a lp, YO, pull through all lps on your hook.

DIRECTIONS
With larger hook, ch 32.
Row 1: Switch to smaller hook, SC in the second ch from your hook, SC in each ch across, turn. 31 sts.
Rows 2-26: Ch 1, MBS in the first st, ch 1, sk the next st, *MBS in next st, ch 1, sk the next st, rep from * across to the last st, MBS in the last st, turn.
Row 27: Ch 1, SC in each st and ch across.

Finishing
Weave in ends, wash, and block to size.

Ebb + Flow

by Jenny Konopinski | 55575

Expanding and contracting, the Ebb + Flow dishcloth uses simple single crochet stitches with intermittent crossed double crochets to create a unique wave effect.

FINISHED MEASUREMENTS
9" square

YARN
CotLin™ (DK weight, 70% Tanguis Cotton, 30% Linen, 123 yards/50g): MC Whisker 24834, C1 Canary 24837, 1 skein each

HOOKS
US F/5 (3.75 mm) Crochet hook or size needed to obtain gauge

NOTIONS
Yarn Needle
Scissors

GAUGE
4 sts = 1" in Single Crochet, blocked

Special Stitches
Crossed Double Crochet (CDC)
Sk next st, 1 DC in next st, 1 DC in sk st working over previous DC.

DIRECTIONS
With MC, Loosely ch 41.

Setup Row 1: SC in third ch from hook, SC in each ch to end, turn.

Setup Row 2: Ch 1 (counts as SC), sk 1 st, SC into each st to end working last st into Tch, turn.

After working the two setup rows, start the wave stitch pattern.

Break MC and continue with C1.

Rows 1-2: Ch 3 (counts as 1 DC), sk 1 st over next 4 sts, work CDC twice, 1 SC into each of next 10 sts, over next 10 sts, work CDC 5 times, 1 SC into each of next 10 sts, over next 4 sts, work CDC twice, 1 DC into Tch, turn.

Break C1 and continue with MC.

Rows 3-4: Ch 1 (counts as SC), sk 1 st, SC into each st to end working last st into Tch, turn.

Break MC and continue with C1.

Rows 5-6: Ch 1 (counts as SC), sk 1 st, SC into each of the next 4 sts, over next 10 sts, work CDC 5 times, 1 SC into each of next 10 sts, over next 10 sts work CDC 5 times, 1 SC into each of last 5 sts working last st into Tch, turn.

Break C1 and continue with MC.

Rows 7-8: Ch 1 (counts as 1 SC), sk 1 st, 1 SC into next and each st to end working last st into Tch, turn.

Rep Rows 1-8 until dishcloth measures 9" long.

Finishing
Weave in ends, wash, and block to size.

Alpine Stitch

by Regan Nishikawa | 58322

The Alpine Stitch creates a nubby, textured dishcloth that is great for adding extra scrubbing power. Alpine stitch is made of a simple repeat that you will memorize quickly, which means it's a great project to work on while you're watching movies or your mind is otherwise occupied.

FINISHED MEASUREMENTS
9" square

YARN
Dishie™ (worsted weight, 100% Cotton, 190 yards/100g): Kenai 25788, 1 skein

HOOKS
US I/9 (5.5mm) Crochet hook or size needed to obtain gauge

NOTIONS
Yarn Needle
Scissors

GAUGE
12 sts and 10 rows = 4" over Alpine Stitch, blocked

Special Stitches

Alpine Stitch Pattern (worked flat)
The Alpine Stitch is composed of one row alternating between DC and FPDC worked over the SC row and into the previous DC row, followed by a row of SC.

DIRECTIONS
Ch 26 sts.
Row 1 (WS): DC in second chain from hook (counts as DC here and throughout), DC across, turn. 24 DC.
Row 2 (RS): Ch 2, DC in each st across, turn.
Row 3: Ch 1, SC in each st across, turn.
Row 4: Ch 2, DC in first 2 sts, *FPDC around next st into previous DC row, DC in next st; rep from * across to last 2 sts, DC in last 2 sts, turn. 14 DC, 10 FPDC.
Row 5: Ch 1, SC in each st across, turn.
Row 6: Ch 2, DC in first 2 sts, *DC in next st, FPDC around next st in previous DC row; rep from * across to last 2 sts, DC in last 2 sts, turn.
Rows 7-22: Rep Rows 3-6.
Row 23: Ch 2, DC in each st across, turn.

Border
Ch 1, SC around working 3 sts into each corner. Fasten off.

Finishing
Weave in ends, wash, and block to size.

Ribbon Candy

by Kim Cameron | 55551

Ribbon Candy dishcloth is a simple combination of single and double crochet stitches with color changes to give it a delicious, textural look. The results give the impression of old fashion ribbon candy. Use two colors or many colors from your stash to create the perfect addition to your kitchen.

FINISHED MEASUREMENTS
9" square

YARN
Dishie™ (worsted weight, 100% Cotton, 190 yards/100g): MC Coffee 25399, C1 Conch 25411, 1 skein each

HOOKS
US G/6 (4.25mm) Crochet hook or size needed to obtain gauge

NOTIONS
Yarn Needle
Scissors

GAUGE
15 sts and 15 rows = 4" over Single Crochet

Notes
When changing colors, on the final stitch, when drawing through the last two lps, use the new yarn color, then ch 1 with the new color. This creates a cleaner change over.

DIRECTIONS
With MC, ch 35.
Row 1: SC in second ch from hook, SC across, turn. 34 SC.
Rows 2-3: Ch 1, SC across, turn.
Row 4: Ch 1, SC across, turn.

Ribbon Stitch
Row 5: With C1 ch 1, * SC, DC, * rep across ending with a DC, turn.
Row 6: Ch 1, * SC Blp, DC, * rep across, turn.
Rows 7-8: With MC, rep Row 2.
Row 9: Rep Row 4.

Rep Rows 5-9 four more times.

Rep Rows 5-6.

Rep Row 2 four times.
Fasten off.

Finishing
Weave in ends, wash, and block to size.

Textured Comb

by Tian Connaughton | 56039

This dishcloth uses a textured, honeycomb-inspired stitch pattern to create a pretty and effective piece to use in the kitchen.

FINISHED MEASUREMENTS
9" wide x 8.5" high

YARN
Dishie™ (worsted weight, 100% Cotton, 190 yards/100g): Swan 24134, 1 skein

HOOKS
US F/5 (3.75mm) Crochet hook or size needed to obtain gauge

NOTIONS
Yarn Needle
Scissors

GAUGE
19 sts = 4" in pattern

DIRECTIONS

Ch 41.

Row 1: Sl st in second ch from hook and next 4 ch, (HDC in next 5 ch, sl st in next 5 ch) 3 times, HDC in last 5 sts, turn. 40 sts.

Row 2: Ch 2, (HDC in Blp in next 5 sts, sl st in Blp in next 5 sts) 4 times, turn.

Row 3: Ch 2, (HDC in Blp in next 5 sts, sl st in Blp in next 5 sts) 4 times, turn.

Row 4: Ch 1, (sl st in Blp in next 5 sts, HDC in Blp in next 5 sts) 4 times, turn.

Row 5: Ch 1, (sl st in Blp in next 5 sts, HDC in Blp in next 5 sts) 4 times, turn.

Row 6: Ch 2, (HDC in Blp in next 5 sts, sl st in Blp in next 5 sts) 4 times, turn.

Rep Rows 3-6 until cloth measures 9" long, do not turn.

Next Rnd: Ch 10, sl st in both lp of same st, working in both lps, SC around, working 3 SC in each corner, sl st in base of beg ch-10.

Finishing
Weave in ends, wash, and block to size.

Misty Rose

by Kim Cameron | 55594

Misty Rose is a fanciful and functional dishcloth to decorate your kitchen. Plus, it's functional! Pick two colors to create a blossom of your own. This pattern is fairly quick to crochet and perfect to give as a gift.

FINISHED MEASUREMENTS
9" diameter

YARN
Dishie™ (worsted weight, 100% Cotton, 190 yards/100g): MC Conch 25411, C1 Silver 25789, 1 skein each

HOOKS
US H/8 (5mm) Crochet hook or size needed to obtain gauge

NOTIONS
Yarn Needle
Scissors

GAUGE
16 sts = 4" over Half Double Crochet, unblocked

DIRECTIONS
Body
Rnd 1: With MC, ch 3 (counts as DC throughout), 7 DC in first ch made, sl st to top of ch 3. 8 sts.
Rnd 2: Ch 2, HDC in same sp, *2 DC in next st, *rep around, sl st to top of ch 2. 16 sts.
Rnd 3: Ch 5, sk one st, sl st in next st, *ch 5, sk one st, sl st in next st *rep around, sl st to top of ch 5. 8 ch-5 sps.
Rnd 4: Sl st into first ch-5 sp, ch 3, 4 DC in same ch-5 sp, *5 DC in next ch-5 sp, rep from * around, sl st to top of ch 3. 40 sts.
Rnd 5: Ch 2 (counts as HDC throughout), 2 HDC in next st, *4 HDC, 2 HDC in next st; * rep around to the last 3 sts, HDC in next 3 sts, sl st to top of ch 2. 48 sts.
Rnd 6: *Ch 5, sk one st, sl st in the next st. *rep around, sl st to the base of the first ch 5. 24 ch-5 sps.
Rnd 7: Sl st into the first ch-5 sp, ch 2, 2 HDC in same ch-5 sp, * 3 DC in next ch-5 sp, rep from * around, sl st to top of ch 2. 72 sts.
Rnd 8: Ch 2, 2 HDC in next st, *8 HDC, 2 HDC in next st continue around to last set, 7 HDC, sl st to top of ch 2. 80 sts.
Rnd 9: *Ch 5, sk one st, sl st in next st, rep from * across, sl st to top of ch 5, fasten off. 40 lps.

Ruffles
Rnd 1: With C1, join in one of the sk sts from Rnd 3, ch 3, 4 DC in same sp, *7 DC in next sk st, rep from * around, sl st to top of ch 3.
Rnd 2: With C1, join in one of the sk sts from Rnd 6, ch 3, 4 HDC in same st, *5 HDC in next sk st, rep from * around, sl st to top of ch 2.
Rnd 3: With C1, but behind the existing lps, join in one of the sk sts from Rnd 9, *ch 6, sl st in next sk st, * rep around, join at the base of the first ch 6.
(Note: an easy way to get to the sk st is to fold the lps of Rnd 9 towards to front to expose the st.)

Finishing
Weave in ends, wash, and block to size.

Golden Lattice
by Hannah Maier | 55597

This is a wonderfully open dishcloth with a sturdy border to draw everything together. The bright, golden color will bring a wonderful cheer to your kitchen and make that pile of dishes seem easier to tackle!

FINISHED MEASUREMENTS
9.5" wide x 9" high

YARN
CotLin™ (DK weight, Tanguis Cotton, 30% Linen, 123 yards/50g): Canary 24837, 1 skein

HOOKS
US F/5 (3.75mm) Crochet hook or size needed to obtain gauge

NOTIONS
Yarn Needle
Scissors

GAUGE
15 HDC = 4"

DIRECTIONS
Ch 45.
Row 1: HDC in fourth ch from hook, (ch 3, HDC in fourth ch, ch 1, sk 1, HDC in next ch) rep 5 more times, ch 3, HDC in last 2 ch sts.
Row 2: Ch 1, SC in first st (ch 2, 3 DC in ch-3 sp, ch 2, SC in ch-1 sp, ch 2) rep to end, SC in Tch of previous row.
Row 3: Ch 5, (HDC in first DC, ch 1, HDC in last DC, ch 3) rep to end, ch 1, tr in last SC st.
Row 4: Ch 3, DC in ch sp, ch 2, (SC in ch sp, ch 2, 3 DC in ch-3 sp, ch 2) rep across, 2 DC in top of ch-5 of previous row.
Row 5: Ch 2, HDC in second DC, (ch 3, HDC in first DC, ch 1, HDC in last DC) to end, 2 HDC in last DC and ch of previous row.

Rep Rows 2-5 until piece measures 8" long, ending with a Row 2 or 4 (whichever gets you closest to 8").

Edging
3 HDC in each corner st, 2 HDC in each ch-3 and tr section of edge, 1 HDC in each DC and SC area of edge around.

2 HDC in each of the four corners, 1 HDC in each HDC around. Break yarn and fasten off.

Finishing
Weave in ends, wash, and block to size.

Golden Lattice Chart

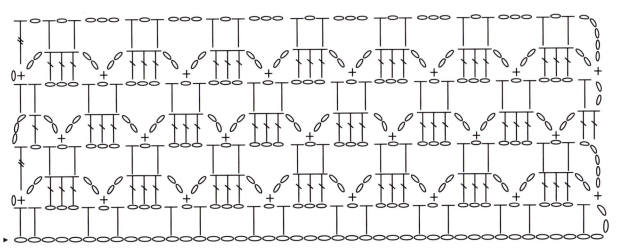

Legend

Cookies & Cream

by Heidi Wells | 55595

Much like the experience of eating a cookie, this dishcloth pattern is sweet, easy and enjoyable. Simple rows of half double crochet in alternating colors are worked up in a jiffy, leaving you plenty of time to finish that cookie snack.

FINISHED MEASUREMENTS
6.5" square

YARN
CotLin™ (DK weight, 70% Tanguis Cotton, 30% Linen, 123 yards/50g): MC Black 24468, C1 Swan 24134, 1 skein each

HOOKS
US I/9 (5.5mm) Crochet hook or size needed to obtain gauge

NOTIONS
Yarn Needle
Scissors

GAUGE
12 HDC = 4"

DIRECTIONS
With MC, Ch 27 (or any number of sts +2).
Row 1: HDC in third ch from hook, HDC across, turn.
Row 2: Ch 2 (does not count as st), HDC in first st, HDC across, turn.

Rep Row 2 until you have a total of 6 rows of MC.

Row 7: With C1 ch 2, HDC across, turn.
Row 8: With MC ch 2, HDC across, turn.
Rows 9-12: Rep Rows 7 & 8.
Row 13: Ch 2, HDC across, turn.

Rep Row 13 until you have 6 rows of MC, fasten off.

Finishing
Weave in ends, wash, and block to size.

Glacial Spa

by Beth Major | 55852

Pretty and practical, this spa cloth uses basic crochet stitches to form an off-set shell stitch pattern to create its simple yet elegant design.

FINISHED MEASUREMENTS
11" square

YARN
Shine™ (sport weight, 60% Pima Cotton, 40% Modal® natural beech wood fiber, 110 yards/50g): Sky 23621, 1 skein

HOOKS
US G/6 (4mm) Crochet hook or size needed to obtain gauge

NOTIONS
Yarn Needle
Scissors

GAUGE
16 sts and 8 rows = 4" in Double Crochet, blocked

Special Stitches

Foundation Single Crochet (FSC)
Ch 2, insert hook in second ch from hook, YO, pull up a lp, YO, pull through 1 lp on hook (ch made), YO, pull through 2 lps (first FSC made), *insert hook into the ch made at the base of the st, YO, pull up a lp, YO, pull through 1 lp on hook (ch made), YO, pull through 2 lps (second FSC made). Rep from * until you have the desired number of sts.

DIRECTIONS
Row 1: FSC 41.
Row 2: Ch 1, turn, (SC, 2 DC, tr) in first st, sk next 3 sts, *(SC, 2 DC, tr) in next st, sk next 3 sts* rep across row, SC in last st.
Row 3: Ch 1, turn, (SC, 2 DC, tr) in first SC, sk next 3 sts, *(SC, 2 DC, tr) in next SC, sk next 3 sts* rep across row, SC in last st.

Rep Row 3 until cloth measures about 10" long.

Finishing
Rnd 1: Ch 1, turn, SC in each st across, 3 SC in last SC of row, work 41 SC along edge, 3 SC in next corner, work SC in each st across, 3 SC in next corner, work 41 SC along last edge, 3 SC in last corner, join last st to first st with a sl st, and fasten off.

Weave in ends, wash, and block to size.

Mismatched

by Stacey Winklepleck | 55560

This dishcloth pattern includes both waves and chevrons with mismatched stripes for a unique look. In this pattern, you will simply switch colors every two rows; using four colors will give you a wave in each color, but this is an easy pattern to customize to as many or as few colors as you would like.

FINISHED MEASUREMENTS
8.5" wide x 9" high

YARN
Dishie™ (worsted weight, 100% Cotton; 190 yards/100g): C1 Mulberry 25784, C2 Verdigris 28098, C3 Blue 25787, C4 Azure 25412, 1 skein each

HOOKS
US 7 (4.5mm) Crochet hook or size needed to obtain gauge

NOTIONS
Yarn Needle
Scissors

GAUGE
14 sts = 4" over Single Crochet

Special Stitches

Single Crochet 2 Together (SC2tog)
(Insert hook in next st, YO, pull up a lp) 2 times (3 lps on hook), YO, draw through all 3 lps on hook.

Single Crochet 3 Together (SC3tog)
(Insert hook in next st, YO, pull up a lp) 3 times (4 lps on hook), YO, draw through all 4 lps on hook.

Treble Crochet 2 Together (tr2tog)
(YO twice, insert hook into next st, YO, pull through 2 lps, YO, pull through 2 lps) 2 times. (3 lps on hook), YO, draw yarn through all 3 lps on hook.

Treble Crochet 3 Together (tr3tog)
(YO twice, insert hook into next st, YO, pull through 2 lps, YO, pull through 2 lps) 3 times. (4 lps on hook), YO, draw yarn through all 4 lps on hook.

DIRECTIONS
With C1, ch 32.

Setup Row (RS): SC in second ch from hook (counts as SC), SC in each ch across, turn.

Row 1 (WS): Ch 1 (counts as SC), sk 1 st *HDC in next st, DC in next st, 3 tr in next st, 1 DC in next st, HDC in next st, SC in next st; rep from * to end, turn.

Row 2: With C2, ch 1, skip 1 st, SC in next st (counts as SC2tog), SC in each of next 2 sts, *3 SC in next st, SC in each of the next 2 st, SC3tog, SC in each of the next 2 sts; rep from * to last 2 sts, work SC2tog over last 2 sts, turn.

Row 3: Rep Row 2.

Row 4: With C3, ch 4, sk 1 st, tr into next st (counts as tr2tog), *DC into next st, HDC in next st, SC in next st, HDC in next st, DC in next st, tr3tog, rep from * to last 2 st, tr2tog, skip Tch, turn.

Row 5: Ch 1 (counts as SC), sk 1, SC in each st to end, turn.

Row 6: With C4, rep Row 5.

Rep Rows 1-6 three more times, remembering to switch colors every two rows and ending after Row 6.

Last Row: Ch 1 (counts as SC), sk 1, SC in each st to end, fasten off.

Finishing
Weave in ends, wash, and block to size.

Creamsicle

by Sarah Nairalez | 58324

Textured stitches are a favorite for dishcloths. Using a Puff Stitch in a checkerboard configuration not only looks visually pleasing but also adds extra texture to your dishcloth.

FINISHED MEASUREMENTS
10" square

YARN
Dishie™ (worsted weight, 100% Cotton, 190 yards/100g): C1 Swan 25409, C2 Clementine 25403, 1 skein each

HOOKS
US E/4 (3.5mm) Crochet hook or size needed to obtain gauge

NOTIONS
Yarn Needle
Scissors

GAUGE
10 sts and 12 rows = 4"

Special Stitches
Puff Stitch (PS)
YO, insert hook in indicated st, YO, pull up a lp to the same height as surrounding sts (3 lps on hook), (YO, insert hook in same st, YO, pull up a lp to the same height as surrounding sts) 4 times (11 lps on hook), YO, pull through all 11 lps.

DIRECTIONS
With C1, ch 44.
Row 1: With C1 and working over C2, HDC in second ch from hook with C1, *ch 1, sk 1, HDC in next, rep from * across. 43 sts.
Row 2: With C1 and carrying C2, ch 2 (counts as HDC here and throughout), HDC in ch sp, ch 1, *switch to C2, PS in next ch sp, with C1 and carrying C2 ch 1, HDC in next ch sp, rep from * across to last st, HDC last st, turn.
Row 3: With C1, ch 2, *HDC into ch sp, ch 1, rep from * across, turn.
Row 4: With C1, ch 2, *HDC into the ch sp 1 row below picking up carried C2, ch 1, with C2, PS into the ch sp below picking up C2, with C1, ch 1 with C1, rep until end across, turn.

*Rep Rows 2-5 until cloth measures approximately 10" long, finish with Row 4. Do not fasten off. Do not turn.

Edging
With C1, ch 1, sl st across top, ch 2 to turn the corner, SC across, ch 2 to turn the corner, sl st across bottom, ch 2, SC across, join with sl st into ch 1.

Finishing
Weave in ends, wash, and block to size.

Orbital

by Stacey Winklepleck | 55542

This is an easy crochet pattern, perfect for beginners looking to move past granny squares. You will only need to know magic circle, double crochet, half double crochet, and increasing. For a solid-colored dishcloth, work every round in the same color. For a striped dishcloth, switch colors at the start of each round. Stitches are worked between the stitches of the previous row, not into the stitches.

FINISHED MEASUREMENTS
10.5" diameter

YARN
Dishie™ (worsted weight, 100% Cotton, 190 yards/100g): Jalapeño 25785, Honeydew 25410, 1 skein each

HOOKS
US 7 (4.5mm) Crochet hook or size needed to obtain gauge

NOTIONS
Yarn Needle
Scissors

GAUGE
4 sts = 1" over Double Crochet

DIRECTIONS

Setup Rnd: Create a large Magic Circle, SC, DC 12, join to first DC with sl st, tighten circle. 12 sts.
Rnd 1: Ch 3 (counts as first DC throughout pattern), DC in same sp, *DC twice in next sp, rep from * until end of rnd, join with sl st to first DC. 24 sts.
Rnd 2: Ch 3, DC in same sp, DC in next sp *DC twice in next sp, DC once in next sp, rep from * until end of rnd, join with sl st to first DC. 36 sts.
Rnd 3: Ch 3, DC in same sp, DC in next 2 sp, *DC twice in next sp, DC in next 2 sp, rep from * until end of rnd, join with sl st to first DC. 48 sts.
Rnd 4: Ch 3, DC around, join with sl st to first DC. 48 sts.
Rnd 5: Ch 3, DC in same sp, DC in next 3 sp, *DC twice in next sp, DC in next 3 sp, rep from * until end of rnd, join with sl st to first DC. 60 sts.
Rnd 6: Ch 3, DC in same sp, DC in next 4 sp, *DC twice in next sp, DC in next 4 sp, rep from * until end of rnd, join with sl st to first DC. 72 sts.
Rnd 7: Ch 3, DC in same sp, DC in next 5 sp, *DC twice in next sp, DC in next 5 sp, rep from * until end of rnd, join with sl st to first DC. 84 sts.
Rnd 8: Ch 3, DC around, join with sl st to first DC. 84 sts.
Rnd 9: Ch 3, DC in same sp, DC in next 6 sp, *DC twice in next sp, DC in next 6 sp, rep from * until end of rnd, join with sl st to first DC. 96 sts.
Rnd 10: Ch 3, DC in same sp, DC in next 7 sp, *DC twice in next sp, DC in next 7 sp, rep from * until end of rnd, join with sl st to first DC. 108 sts.
Rnd 11: Ch 2 (counts as first HDC), HDC around, join with sl st to first HDC. 108 sts.

Finishing
Weave in ends, wash, and block to size.

Dragonfly Delight

by Jennifer Pionk | 56001

Create a dragonfly motif by crocheting in rounds with strategically-placed basic stitches. Add a simple edging in a contrasting color for a clean finishing touch.

FINISHED MEASUREMENTS
6.5" square

YARN
Dishie™ (worsted weight, 100% Cotton, 190 yards/100g): MC Blush 26668, C1 Swan 25409, 1 skein each

HOOKS
US H/8 (5mm) Crochet hook or size needed to obtain gauge

NOTIONS
Yarn Needle
Scissors

GAUGE
12 sts and 6 rows = 3" in Double Crochet

DIRECTIONS
Dragonfly Square
Dragonfly square is worked in MC.

Rnd 1: Begin with a Magic Circle, ch 4 (counts as first DC + ch-1), work the following in the Magic Circle, *3 DC, ch 1, work from * 3 times, then 2 DC. Join with a sl st to the third ch. 12 DC + 4 ch-1 sps.

Rnd 2: Sl st over to first ch-1 sp, ch 4 (counts as first DC + ch-1), 2 DC in same ch-1 sp, *DC in each of the next 3 sts, (2 DC, ch 1, 2 DC) in next ch-1 sp, work from * 3 times, then DC in each of the next 3 sts, dc in next ch-1 sp. Join with a sl st to the third ch. 28 DC + 4 ch-1 sps.

Rnd 3: Sl st over to first ch-1 sp, ch 4 (counts as first DC + ch-1), 2 DC in same ch-1 sp, *DC in each of the next 3 sts, ch 1, sk the next st, DC in each of the next 3 sts, (2 DC, ch 1, 2 DC) in next ch-1 sp, work from * 3 times, then DC in each of the next 3 sts, ch 1, sk the next st, DC in each of the next 3 sts, DC in the next ch-1 sp. Join with a sl st to the third ch. 40 DC + 8 ch-1 sps.

Rnd 4: Sl st over to first ch-1 sp, ch 4 (counts as first DC + ch-1), 2 DC in same ch-1 sp, *DC in each of the next 2 sts, ch 3, sk the next 3 sts, SC in the next ch-1 sp, ch 3, sk the next 3 sts, DC in each of the next 2 sts, (2 DC, ch 1, 2 DC) in next ch-1 sp, work from * 3 times, then DC in each of the next 2 sts, ch 3, sk the next 3 sts, SC in the next ch-1 sp, ch 3, sk the next 3 sts, DC in the next 2 sts, DC in the next ch-1 sp. Join with a sl st to the third ch. 36 sts + 4 ch-1 sps + 8 ch-3 sps.

Rnd 5: Sl st over to first ch-1 sp, ch 4 (counts as first DC + ch-1), 2 DC in same ch-1 sp, *DC in each of the next 3 sts, ch 4, sk the next DC and next ch-3 sp, sl st in the next SC, ch 4, sk the next ch-3 sp and DC, DC in each of the next 3 sts, (2 DC, ch 1, 2 DC) in next ch-1 sp, work from * 3 times, then DC in each of the next 3 sts, ch 4, sk the next DC and ch-3 sp, sl st in the next SC, ch 4, sk the next ch-3 sp and DC, DC in each of the next 3 sts, DC in the next ch-1 sp. Join with a sl st to the third ch. 44 sts + 4 ch-1 sps + 8 ch-4 sps.

Rnd 6: Sl st over to first ch-1 sp, ch 4 (counts as first DC + ch-1), 2 DC in same ch-1 sp, *DC in each of the next 5 sts, 4 DC in the next ch-4 sp, tr in the next sl st, 4 DC in the next ch-4 sp, DC in each of the next 5 sts, (2 DC, ch 1, 2 DC) in next ch-1 sp, work from * 3 times, then DC in each of the next 5 sts, 4 DC in the next ch-4 sp, tr in the next sl st, 4 DC in the next ch-4 sp, DC in each of the next 5 sts, DC in the next ch-1 sp. Join with a sl st to the third ch. 92 sts + 4 ch-1 sps.

Break MC.

Edging
Rnd 1: With C1, ch 1, *(SC, ch 2, SC, ch 2, SC) in the next ch-1 sp, SC in each of the next 23 sts, rep from * around. Join with a sl st to the first st. 104 sts + 8 ch-2 sps.

Finishing
Weave in ends, wash, and block to size.

Peach Margot

by Hannah Maier | 55555

These bright, spring colors add some pop to the traditional Catherine Wheel crochet stitch. It's also a great chance to practice your cluster stitch skills!

FINISHED MEASUREMENTS
8" square

YARN
CotLin™ (DK weight, 70% Tanguis Cotton, 30% Linen, 123 yards/50g): MC Flamingo 25322, C1 Conch 25776, 1 skein each

HOOKS
US G/6 (4mm) Crochet hook or size needed to obtain gauge

NOTIONS
Yarn Needle
Scissors

GAUGE
17 sts and 24 rows = 4" over Single Crochet

Special Stitches
Cluster Stitch (CL)
(YO, insert hook, YO, draw lp through, YO, draw through two lps) over indicated sts, YO, draw through all lps on hook.

DIRECTIONS
With MC ch 47.
Row 1 (WS): SC into second ch from hook, SC into next ch, (sk 3 ch, 7 DC into next ch, sk 3 ch, SC into next 3 ch) rep to last 4 ch, sk 3 ch, 4 DC into last ch, turn.
Row 2 (RS): With C1 ch 1, SC into first 2 sts (ch 3, CL over next 7 sts, ch 3, SC into next 3 sts) rep to last 4 sts, ch 3, 1 CL over last 4 sts, sk Tch, turn.
Row 3: Ch 3 (counts as DC here and throughout), 3 DC into first st (sk ch-3 sp, SC into next 3 SC, sk ch-3 sp, 7 DC into closing lp of next CL) rep until end finishing with a sk ch-3 sp, SC into last 2 sts.
Row 4: With MC ch 3, sk first st, CL over next 3 sts (ch 3, SC int next 3 sts, ch 3, CL over next 7 sts) rep to end, finishing with ch 3, SC into next st and Tch.
Row 5: Ch 1, SC into first two sts (sk ch-3 sp, 7 DC into closing loop of next CL, sk ch-3 sp, SC into next 3 SC) rep to end, finishing with sk ch-3 sp, 4 DC into tch, turn.
Rep Rows 2-5 four more times, work one more Row 2.

Finishing
Weave in ends, wash, and block to size.

Celtic Weave

by Tian Connaughton | 55034

The Celtic Weave dishcloth features a textured stitch that creates a surface perfect for scrubbing.

FINISHED MEASUREMENTS
10" square

YARN
Dishie™ Multi (worsted weight, 100% Cotton, 190 yards/100g): Sunshine 27341, 1 skein

HOOKS
US G/6 (4mm) Crochet hook or size needed to obtain gauge

NOTIONS
Yarn Needle
Scissors

GAUGE
19 sts and 15 rows = 4" in pattern

Special Stitches

FPtr (Front post treble crochet)
YO twice, insert hook around post of indicated st from front to back to front, YO pull up a lp (4 lps on hook), (YO, pull through 2 lps) 3 times.

BPtr (Back post treble crochet)
YO twice, insert hook around post of indicated st from back to front to back, YO pull up a lp (4 lps on hook), (YO, pull through 2 lps) 3 times.

DIRECTIONS
Ch 39.

Row 1: HDC in second ch from hook and in each st across row, turn. 38 sts.

Row 2: Ch 1, HDC in each st across row, turn.

Row 3: Ch 1, HDC in first st, *sk next 2 sts, FPtr around post of next 2 st, working behind last 2 tr just made, BPtr in 2 skipped sts; rep from * to last st, HDC, turn.

Row 4: Ch 1, SC in each st across row, turn.

Row 5: Ch 1, HDC in first 3 sts, *sk next 2 sts, FPtr around post of next 2 FPtr 2 rows below, working in front of last 2 sts just made, FPtr around post of skipped 2 BPtr 2 rows below; rep from * across to last 3 sts, HDC in next 3 sts.

Row 6: Ch 1, SC in each st across row, turn.

Row 7: Ch 1, HDC in first st, sk next 2 sts, FPtr around post of next 2 BPtr, working behind last 2 tr just made, BPtr around post of 2 skipped HDC sts 2 rows below, *sk next 2 sts, FPtr around post of next 2 BPtr, working behind last 2 tr just made, BPtr around post of skipped FPtr; rep from * to 5 last sts, sk next 2 sts, FPtr around post of next 2 HDC sts 2 rows below, working behind last 2 tr just made, BPtr around post of 2 skipped HDC sts 2 rows below, HDC in last st, turn.

Row 8: Ch 1, SC in each st across row, turn.

Rep Rows 5-8 until cloth measures 9.5" long.

Next Row: Ch 1, SC in each st across row.
Fasten off.

Finishing
Weave in ends, wash, and block to size.

Tunisian Purl Stitch

by Tian Connaughton | 56056

Use simple Tunisian stitches to create this fun and quick dishcloth with edges and a hanging loop. The bumpy texture is perfect for scrubbing dishes. Use solid colors or multi—either way, you'll have a wonderful and useful project for your kitchen.

FINISHED MEASUREMENTS
9" square, not including edge

YARN
Dishie™ Multi (worsted weight, 100% Cotton, 190 yards/100g): Aquarium 27340, 1 skein

HOOKS
US J/10 (6mm) Tunisian hook or size needed to obtain gauge
US G/6 (4mm) Crochet hook or size needed to obtain gauge

NOTIONS
Yarn Needle
Scissors

GAUGE
16 sts and 12 rows = 4" in pattern

Special Stitches

Tunisian Purl Stitch (TPS) [forward pass]
Sk first vertical bar, bring yarn to front, insert hook in next vertical bar, bring yarn to back under hook, wrap around hook from back to front, draw yarn through st (purl made).

DIRECTIONS
Ch 36.
Foundation Row (forward pass): Keeping all lps on hook, sk first ch from hook (the lp on the hook is the first ch) and draw up a lp in each ch across row, do not turn.
Foundation Row (return pass): YO, draw through first lp on hook, *YO, draw through next 2 lps; rep from * across row until 1 lp rem on hook (the lp rem on the hook always counts as the first st of the next row).
Row 1 (forward pass): Sk first st, *TPS in each st across row, do not turn.
Row 1 (return pass): YO, draw through 1 lp, (this ch forms the edge st), *YO, draw through 2 lps; rep from * until 1 lp rem on hook (the lp left on the hook is the first st of the next row), do not turn.
Rep Row 1 forward pass and return pass until cloth measures 9" long from beg ch.

Remove Tunisian hook from lp and replace with crochet hook. Beg working in HDC around as follows: ch 2, HDC in first st across row, 3 HDC in corner, HDC down side, 3 HDC in next corner, HDC in each foundation ch, 3 HDC in corner, HDC in edge up side to corner, ch 10, join with sl st to ch at beg of rnd.
Fasten off.

Finishing
Weave in ends, wash, and block to size.

Nice-n-Easy

by Beth Major | 55839

Create a quick and easy cloth for the spa or the kitchen. This pattern will become your go-to for a last-minute gift.

FINISHED MEASUREMENTS
10" square

YARN
Shine™ (sport weight, 60% Pima Cotton, 40% Modal® natural beech wood fiber, 110 yards/50g):
Hydrangea 23813, 1 skein

HOOKS
US G/6 (4mm) Crochet hook or size needed to obtain gauge

NOTIONS
Yarn Needle
Scissors

GAUGE
9 sts and 10 rows = 2" over Single Crochet

Special Stitches

Reverse SC (or Crab Stitch) (RSC)
Working left to right, insert hook into next st, YO and pull up a lp, YO and pull through both lps on hook.

DIRECTIONS
Ch 43.
Row 1: SC in second ch from hook and each ch across, turn. 42 sts.
Row 2: Ch 1, SC in Blp of each SC across, turn. 42 sts.

Rep Row 2 until cloth measures 10 inches, do not fasten off, do not turn.

Edging
Row 1: Ch 1, work 3 SC into last SC, (evenly sp 42 SC along edge of cloth, 3 SC in next corner) 3 times, SC in each SC across, join with sl st.
Row 2: Ch 1, work RSC in each SC around, join with sl st to Tch, fasten off.

Finishing
Weave in ends, wash, and block to size.

Teal Swirl

by Heidi Wells | 55563

This granny square pattern is the perfect quick and easy dishcloth. Using only double crochet, it's easy to memorize and is great for a beginning crocheter. The transitioning color stripes are easy to customize to your kitchen's color scheme!

FINISHED MEASUREMENTS
10.5" wide x 10" high

YARN
Dishie™ (worsted weight, 100% Cotton; 190 yards/100g): C1 Swan 25409, C2 Honeydew 25410, C3 Verdigris 28098, C4 Kenai 25788, 1 skein each

HOOKS
US J/10 (6mm) Crochet hook or size needed to obtain gauge

NOTIONS
Yarn Needle
Scissors

GAUGE
12 sts = 4" over Double Crochet

DIRECTIONS
With C1, ch 4, join with sl st to form ring.
Rnd 1: Ch 3 (counts as DC here and throughout), 2 DC into ring, ch 2, [3 DC into ring, ch 2] twice, 3 DC into ring, join with HDC to Tch (counts as ch 2).
Rnd 2: Ch 3, DC into same ch sp,* DC in each st across to corner ch sp, (2 DC**, ch 2, 2 DC into ch sp; rep from * twice more, then from * to ** once more, join with HDC into Tch (counts as ch-2). Fasten off. 28 sts, 4 ch sps.
Rnd 3: With C2, rep Rnd 2.
Rnd 4: Rep Rnd 2, fasten off C2.
Rnd 5: With C3, rep Rnd 2.
Rnd 6: Rep Rnd 2, fasten off C3.
Rnd 7: With C4, rep Rnd 2.
Rnd 8: Rep Rnd 2 to **, ch 2, join with sl st into Tch, fasten off C4.

Finishing
Weave in ends, wash, and block to size.

Dancing Shells

by Kim Cameron | 55587

The shell stitch is a popular crochet stitch, however, this dishcloth takes it a step further. The dancing raised shells give an interesting texture to look at while working double duty when washing your dishes!

FINISHED MEASUREMENTS
9" wide x 8.5" high

YARN
Dishie™ (worsted weight, 100% Cotton, 190 yards/100g): Azure 25412, 1 skein

HOOKS
US I/9 (5.5mm) Crochet hook or size needed to obtain gauge

NOTIONS
Yarn Needle
Scissors

GAUGE
14 SC = 4", blocked

Special Stitches

Front Post Double Crochet (FPDC)
YO, insert hook around the post indicated st from front to back to front, YO, pull through, [YO, pull through 2 lps on hook] twice.

DIRECTIONS
Ch 31.
Row 1: SC in second ch from hook, SC across, turn. 30 sts.
Row 2: Ch 3, sk first 2 SC, *3 DC in next SC, sk 1 SC, 1 DC in next SC, sk next SC, rep from * across, 3 DC in last SC, turn.
Row 3: Ch 1, SC in each st across, turn.
Row 4: Ch 3 (counts as DC), *sk next SC, DC in next SC (center st of row below shell), sk next SC, work 3 FPDC around DC 1 row below next SC, rep from * across, 1 DC in last st, turn.
Row 5: Ch 1, SC in each st across, turn.
Row 6: Ch 3 (counts as DC), sk next 2 SC, *3 FPDC around DC 1 row below next SC, sk next SC, DC in center st of the shell below, rep from * across, 1 DC in last st, turn.

Rep Rows 3-6 four more times.

Rep Rows 3-4 once.

Last Row: Ch 1, SC in each st across.

Finishing
Weave in ends, wash, and block to size.

Log Cabin

by Tian Connaughton | 56036

Play with colors, use up scraps with this fun and quick log cabin-inspired dishcloth. Each new color builds off of the squares created before, turning the piece clockwise and working into the ends of each row. Weave in ends as you go.

FINISHED MEASUREMENTS
8.5" square

YARN
CotLin™ (DK weight, 70% Tanguis Cotton, 30% Linen, 123 yards/50g): C1 Copper 27749, C2 Mustard Seed 27750, C3 Thicket 26995, C4 Ivy 26994, C5 Whisker 24834, C6 Cashew 24461, 1 skein each

HOOKS
US F/5 (3.75mm) Crochet hook or size needed to obtain gauge

NOTIONS
Yarn Needle
Scissors

GAUGE
16 sts and 16 rows = 4" in Single Crochet

DIRECTIONS

Square 1
With C1, ch 9.
Row 1: Sk first ch, SC in next 8 ch, turn. 8 sts.
Rows 2-3: Ch 1, SC in each st across row, turn.
Row 4: Ch 1, SC in each st across row. Fasten off.

Square 2
Join C2 to end.
Rows 1-3: Ch 1, SC in each st across row, turn. 8 sts.
Row 4: Ch 1, SC in each st across row. Fasten off.

Square 3
Turn work clockwise to work in side of sts, join C3 to end.
Row 1: Ch 1, SC in end of each row, turn. 8 sts.
Rows 2-3: Ch 1, SC in each st across row, turn. 8 sts.
Row 4: Ch 1, SC in each st across row. Fasten off.

Square 4
Turn work clockwise to work in side of sts, join C4 to end.
Row 1: Ch 1, SC in end of each row, turn. 12 sts.
Rows 2-3: Ch 1, SC in each st across row, turn. 12 sts.
Row 4: Ch 1, SC in each st across row. Fasten off.

Square 5
Turn work clockwise to work in side of sts, join C5 to end.
Row 1: Ch 1, SC in end of each row, turn. 12 sts.
Rows 2-3: Ch 1, SC in each st across row, turn. 12 sts.
Row 4: Ch 1, SC in each st across row. Fasten off.

Square 6
Turn work clockwise to work in side of sts, join C6 to end.
Row 1: Ch 1, SC in end of each row, turn. 16 sts.
Rows 2-3: Ch 1, SC in each st across row, turn. 16 sts.
Row 4: Ch 1, SC in each st across row. Fasten off.

Square 7
Turn work clockwise to work in side of sts, join C1 to end.
Row 1: Ch 1, SC in end of each row, turn. 16 sts.
Rows 2-3: Ch 1, SC in each st across row, turn. 16 sts.
Row 4: Ch 1, SC in each st across row. Fasten off.

Square 8
Turn work clockwise to work in side of sts, join C2 to end.
Row 1: Ch 1, SC in end of each row, turn. 20 sts.
Rows 2-3: Ch 1, SC in each st across row, turn. 20 sts.
Row 4: Ch 1, SC in each st across row. Fasten off.

Square 9
Turn work clockwise to work in side of sts, join C3 to end.
Row 1: Ch 1, SC in end of each row, turn. 20 sts.
Rows 2-3: Ch 1, SC in each st across row, turn. 20 sts.
Row 4: Ch 1, SC in each st across row. Fasten off.

Square 10
Turn work clockwise to work in side of sts, join C4 to end.
Row 1: Ch 1, SC in end of each row, turn. 24 sts.
Rows 2-3: Ch 1, SC in each st across row, turn. 24 sts.
Row 4: Ch 1, SC in each st across row. Fasten off.

Square 11
Turn work clockwise to work in side of sts, join C5 to end.
Row 1: Ch 1, SC in end of each row, turn. 24 sts.
Rows 2-3: Ch 1, SC in each st across row, turn. 24 sts.
Row 4: Ch 1, SC in each st across row. Fasten off.

Square 12
Turn work clockwise to work in side of sts, join C6 to end.
Row 1: Ch 1, SC in end of each row, turn. 28 sts.
Rows 2-3: Ch 1, SC in each st across row, turn. 28 sts.
Row 4: Ch 1, SC in each st across row. Fasten off.

Square 13
Turn work clockwise to work in side of sts, join C1 to end.
Row 1: Ch 1, SC in end of each row, turn. 28 sts.
Rows 2-3: Ch 1, SC in each st across row, turn. 28 sts.
Row 4: Ch 1, SC in each st across row. Fasten off.

Square 14
Turn work clockwise to work in side of sts, join C2 to end.
Row 1: Ch 1, SC in end of each row, turn. 32 sts.
Rows 2-3: Ch 1, SC in each st across row, turn. 32 sts.
Row 4: Ch 1, SC in each st across row. Fasten off.

Turn work clockwise to work in side of sts, join C3 to end.
Next Rnd: Ch 1, (SC in end of each row to last st (31 sts), work 3 SC in corner next) 4 times.

Next 2 Rnds: Ch 1, SC in each st around, working 3 SC in each corner st. Fasten off.

Finishing
Weave in ends, wash, and block to size.

Cabled Spa

by Beth Major | 55821

Learn the basics of crochet cabling with this wonderfully textured spa cloth.

FINISHED MEASUREMENTS
10" square

YARN
CotLin™ (DK weight, 70% Tanguis Cotton, 30% Linen, 123 yards/50g): Coffee 24138, 1 skein

HOOKS
US G/6 (4mm) Crochet hook or size needed to obtain gauge

NOTIONS
Yarn Needle
Scissors

GAUGE
18 sts and 12 rows = 4" over Half Double Crochet, blocked

Special Stitches

Front Post Double Crochet (FPDC)
YO, insert hook front to back to front around indicated st, YO, pull up a lp, [YO, draw through 2 lps on hook] 2 times.

Back Post Double Crochet (BPDC)
YO, insert hook back to front to back around indicated st, YO, pull up a lp, [YO, draw through 2 lps on hook] 2 times.

Front Post Treble Crochet (FPtr)
YO twice, insert hook front to back to front around indicated st, YO, pull up a lp, [YO, draw through 2 lps on hook] 3 times.

DIRECTIONS
Ch 42, turn.

Row 1: DC in fourth ch from hook and in each ch across, turn. 40 DC.

Row 2: Ch 2, HDC in first DC, BPDC around next 2 DC, HDC in next 3 DC, BPDC around next 3 DC, HDC in next 4 DC, BPDC around next 4 DC, HDC in next 2 DC, BPDC around next 2 DC, HDC in next 2 DC, BPDC around next 4 DC, HDC in next 4 DC, BPDC around next 3 DC, HDC in next 3 DC, BPDC around next 2 DC, HDC in last st, turn.

Row 3: Ch 2, HDC in first HDC, sk next BPDC, FPDC around next BPDC and the skipped BPDC, HDC in next 3 HDC, sk next BPDC, FPdc around next 2 BPDC, FPtr around skipped BPDC, HDC in next 4 HDC, sk next 2 BPDC, FPtr around next 2 BPDC then around skipped BPDC, HDC in next 2 HDC, FPDC around next 2 BPDC, HDC in next 2 HDC, sk next 2 BPDC, FPtr around next 2 BPDC then around skipped BPDC, HDC in next 4 HDC, FPDC around next 2 BPDC, FPtr around skipped BPDC, HDC in next 3 HDC, FPDC around next BPDC and the skipped BPDC, HDC in last HDC, turn.

Row 4: Ch 2, HDC in first HDC, BPDC around next 2 FPDC, HDC in next 3 HDC, BPDC around next FPtr and around next 2 FPDC, HDC in next 4 HDC, BPDC around next 4 FPtr, HDC in next 2 HDC, BPDC around next 2 FPDC, HDC in next 2 HDC, BPDC around next 4 FPtr, HDC in next 4 HDC, BPDC around next FPtr and next 2 FPDC, HDC in next 3 HDC, BPDC around next 2 FPDC, HDC in last HDC.

Row 5: Ch 2, turn, HDC in first HDC, BPDC around next 2 FPDC, HDC in next 3 HDC, BPDC around next FPtr and around next 2 FPDC, HDC in next 4 HDC, BPDC around next 4 FPtr, HDC in next 2 HDC, BPDC around next 2 FPdc, HDC in next 2 HDC, BPDC around next 4 FPtr, HDC in next 4 HDC, BPDC around next FPtr and next 2 FPDC, HDC in next 3 HDC, BPDC around next 2 FPDC, HDC in last HDC.

Rep Rows 4 and 5 until cloth measures about 9" long, finishing with a Row 5.

Finishing
C1, do not turn, 2 SC in same st, evenly sp 38 SC along edge, [3 SC in corner, evenly sp 38 SC along next edge] 3 times, join with sl st to first SC, and fasten off.

Weave in ends, wash, and block to size.

Tunisian Lattice

by Sarah Nairalez | 58327

The Tunisian Lattice dishcloth offers simple grace to your dishcloth collection. The thick fabric created by the Tunisian stitches helps make a secure and absorbent dishcloth.

FINISHED MEASUREMENTS
12" square

YARN
Shine™ (worsted weight, 60% Pima Cotton, 40% Modal® natural beech wood fiber, 75 yards/50g): Dandelion 25357, 1 skein

HOOKS
US F/5 (3.75mm) Tunisian Crochet hook or size needed to obtain gauge

NOTIONS
Yarn Needle
Scissors

GAUGE
24 TSS and 17 TSS = 4"

Special Stitches

Tunisian Simple Stitch (TSS) [forward pass]
Insert hook behind the front vertical bar, YO and pull up a lp, leaving the lp on the hook.

Return pass (RetP)
YO, pull through one lp on hook, *YO pull through 2 lps on hook, rep * until one lp is left on hook.

Last Tunisian Stitch (LTS)
Insert hook under both vertical bars of the last st and complete as for TSS.

Tunisian Simple Stitch 2 Together (TSS2tog)
YO, pull through one lp on hook, *YO pull through 2 lps on hook, rep * until one lp is left on hook.

DIRECTIONS
With C1, ch 55.
Row 1: Pull up a lp in the back bump of the second ch from hook and each ch across. RetP.
Row 2: TSS across. RetP.
Row 3: (TSS2tog, TSS in the first st of the TSSt2tog) across last 2 sts, TSS 1, LTS. RetP.
Row 4: TSS 1, (TSSt2tog, TSS in the first st of the TSS2tog) across last st, LTS, RetP.

Rep Rows 3-4 until your square measures 10" long.

Edging
Once you've finished that last row RetP, you can start your edging. Sl st over the top and bottom of the dishcloth, ch to turn the corner, SC on the sides.

Finishing
Weave in ends, wash, and block to size.

The Jerrica

by Jenny Konopinski | 55599

This truly outrageous dishcloth uses simple single crochet throughout and a small amount of embroidery for a quick and fabulous project. You'll feel like a superstar every time you wash the dishes!

FINISHED MEASUREMENTS
7" square

YARN
Comfy™ (worsted weight, 75% Pima Cotton, 25% Acrylic, 109 yards/50g): MC Black 25316, C1 Sea Foam 24153, C2 Zinnia 25770, 1 skein each

HOOKS
US F/3 (3.75mm) Crochet hook or size needed to obtain gauge

NOTIONS
Yarn Needle
Scissors

GAUGE
20 sts = 4" over Single Crochet

DIRECTIONS

Body
With MC, ch 30.
Row 1: SC in second ch from hook, SC across, turn.
Rows 2-32: Ch 1, SC across, turn.
Fasten off after Row 32.

Border
Row 1: With C1, insert hook into a corner sp, (SC, ch 1, SC) in same sp, SC in every SC to next corner, (SC, ch 1, SC) into corner sp, 28 SC alongside the edge to next corner, (SC, ch 1, SC) into corner sp, SC in every SC to next corner, (SC, ch 1, SC) into corner sp, 28 SC alongside the edge, sl st in first SC to join and fasten off.

Cross Stitching Embroidery
Using a long length of C2 and a yarn needle, begin at the bottom right-hand corner of the square with RS facing and insert the needle into the sp of the first st and 1 row from corner. Work cross stitch pattern over 2 sts and 2 rows. Sk 1 row, bring needle up in row above and matching to the cross stitch that was just made. Work next cross stitch and rep up the length of the dishcloth until you are one row from the top.

Rotate dishcloth 180 degrees, sk st and make next row of sts aligned with the last, moving to the bottom edge of the dishcloth.

Rep until the dishcloth is covered, leaving a sp of one row at the top and bottom, and one st at either side. Fasten off.

Finishing
Weave in ends, wash, and block to size.

Berry Jam Jar

by Sarah Nairalez | 58323

Add some flavor to your kitchen using Berry Stitch to create mini textured berries in this dishcloth pattern. The Berry Stitches stack neatly on top of each other for a classic look, and are great for scrubbing dishes.

FINISHED MEASUREMENTS
10" square

YARN
Dishie™ (worsted weight, 100% Cotton, 190 yards/100g): C1 Swan 25409, C2 Fiesta Red 25786, 1 skein each

HOOKS
US E/4 (3.5mm) Crochet hook or size needed to obtain gauge

NOTIONS
Yarn Needle
Scissors

GAUGE
18 sts and 10 rows = 4" over stitch pattern

Special Stitches

Berry Stitch
YO, insert hook in indicated st, YO, pull up lp, YO, pull through one lp, YO, insert hook in same st, YO, pull up lp through, YO, pull all 5 lps on the hook.

DIRECTIONS
With C1, ch 44.
Row 1: While working over C2 SC in second ch from hook and in each ch across, turn. 43 SC.
Row 2: With C1, ch 1, *SC in first st, with C2, Berry Stitch; rep from * to last 2 sts, with C1 SC in the last sts, turn.
Row 3: With C1, ch 1, while working over C2, SC in each st across, turn. 43 SC.

Rep Rows 2-3 until piece measures approximately 10" square ending with Row 3. Do not fasten off.

Edging
Continuing with C1, ch 1, and sl st across the row, ch 2 to turn the corner and SC down the edge, ch 2 to turn the corner, sl st across the bottom, ch 2, and SC up that last side. Fasten off.

Finishing
Weave in ends, wash, and block to size.

Étoile

by Jenny Konopinski | 55561

Étoile adorns simple stripes with a fun star stitch—this not only adds a bit of texture to the dishcloth, but adds pops of color against the contrasting stripes. Worked primarily in single crochet, and is great for using up yarn from your stash.

FINISHED MEASUREMENTS
7.5" wide x 8" high

YARN
CotLin™ (DK weight, 70% Tanguis Cotton, 30% Linen, 123 yards/50g): MC Swan 24134, C1 Wallaby 25775, 1 skein each

HOOKS
US G/6 (4mm) Crochet hook or size needed to obtain gauge

NOTIONS
Yarn Needle
Scissors

GAUGE
5 sts = 1" in Single Crochet

Special Stitches

Star Stitch Cluster (CL)
For this stitch, you will be picking up 5 lps by inserting your hook as follows: 2 sts to right of next st and 1 row down, 1 st to right of next st and 2 rows down, directly below next st and 3 rows down, 1 st to left of next st and 2 down, 2 sts to left of next st and 1 row down. There will be 6 lps on your hook. Now insert your hook into the top of the next st, YO, draw lp through, YO, and then draw through all 7 sts on hook.

DIRECTIONS
With MC loosely ch 36.
Row 1: SC in second ch from hook and across, turn. 35 sts.
Row 2: Ch 1, SC across, turn. 35 sts.
Rows 3-10: Ch 1, rep Row 2, change to C1, turn. 35 sts.
Star Stitch Stripe 1: Ch 1, SC in next 5 sts, *CL, 7 SC, rep from * 2 more times, CL, SC in last 5 sts, turn. 35 sts.
Row 12: Rep Row 2 five more times, change to MC, turn. 35 sts.
Star Stitch Stripe 2: Ch 1, SC in next 9 sts, *CL, 7 SC, rep from * one more time, CL, SC in last 9 sts, turn. 35 sts.
Row 18: Rep Row 2 five times, change to C1, turn.

Rep Start Stitch Stripe 1 to Row 18 one more time.
Next Row: With MC, SC across.

Rep Next Row nine more times. Fasten off.

Finishing
Weave in ends, wash, and block to size.

Hipacious Houndstooth

by Jennifer Pionk | 56002

Add a hip spin to the classic houndstooth stitch pattern. Instead of the traditional black and white, try using your two favorite colors to create this updated version.

FINISHED MEASUREMENTS
7" square

YARN
Dishie™ (worsted weight, 100% Cotton, 190 yards/100g): MC Conch 25411, C1 Mint 27041, 1 skein each

HOOKS
US H/8 (5mm) Crochet hook or size needed to obtain gauge
US I/9 (5.5mm) Crochet hook or size needed to obtain gauge

NOTIONS
Yarn Needle
Scissors

GAUGE
15 sts and 14 rows = 4" in pattern

Notes
Work all odd-numbered rows MC.
Work all even-numbered rows in C1.
Beg ch-1 does not count as a st.

DIRECTIONS
With larger hook and MC, ch 27.
Row 1: Change to smaller hook, SC in the second ch from hook, DC in the next ch, *SC in the next ch, DC in the next ch, rep from * across, turn. 26 sts.
Row 2: Ch 1, *SC in the next DC, DC in the next SC, rep from * across, turn.

Rep Row 2 until dishcloth measures 7" long.

Finishing
Weave in ends, wash, and block to size.

Mitered Square

by Tian Connaughton | 56037

This crochet dishcloth is quick to make, and takes full advantage of the shifting colors on the multi yarn. Two stitches are decreased at the end of the cloth every row, and ends with a round of half double crochet and a loop for hanging.

FINISHED MEASUREMENTS
9.25" square

YARN
Dishie™ Multi (worsted weight, 100% Cotton, 190 yards/100g): Deep Blue Sea 27338, 1 skein

HOOKS
US H/8 (5mm) Crochet hook or size needed to obtain gauge

NOTIONS
Yarn Needle
Scissors

GAUGE
12 sts and 8 rows = 4" in pattern

Special Stitches

HDC3tog
YO, insert hook in first st, YO, pull up a lp (3 lps on hook), YO, insert hook in next st, YO, pull up a lp (5 lps on hook), YO, insert hook in third st, YO, pull up a lp (7 lps on hook), YO, pull through all 7 lps.

DIRECTIONS
Ch 58.
Row 1: HDC in second ch from hook and in each st across row, turn. 57 sts.
Row 2: Ch 1, HDC in next 27 sts, HDC3tog, HDC in next 27 sts, turn. 55 sts.
Row 3: Ch 1, HDC in next 26 sts, HDC3tog, HDC in next 26 sts, turn. 53 sts.
Row 4: Ch 1, HDC in next 25 sts, HDC3tog, HDC in next 25 sts, turn. 51 sts.
Row 5: Ch 1, HDC in next 24 sts, HDC3tog, HDC in next 24 sts, turn. 49 sts.
Row 6: Ch 1, HDC in next 23 sts, HDC3tog, HDC in next 23 sts, turn. 47 sts.
Row 7: Ch 1, HDC in next 22 sts, HDC3tog, HDC in next 22 sts, turn. 45 sts.
Row 8: Ch 1, HDC in next 21 sts, HDC3tog, HDC in next 21 sts, turn. 43 sts.
Row 9: Ch 1, HDC in next 20 sts, HDC3tog, HDC in next 20 sts, turn. 41 sts.
Row 10: Ch 1, HDC in next 19 sts, HDC3tog, HDC in next 19 sts, turn. 39 sts.
Row 11: Ch 1, HDC in next 18 sts, HDC3tog, HDC in next 18 sts, turn. 37 sts.
Row 12: Ch 1, HDC in next 17 sts, HDC3tog, HDC in next 17 sts, turn. 35 sts.
Row 13: Ch 1, HDC in next 16 sts, HDC3tog, HDC in next 16 sts, turn. 33 sts.
Row 14: Ch 1, HDC in next 15 sts, HDC3tog, HDC in next 15 sts, turn. 31 sts.
Row 15: Ch 1, HDC in next 14 sts, HDC3tog, HDC in next 14 sts, turn. 29 sts.
Row 16: Ch 1, HDC in next 13 sts, HDC3tog, HDC in next 13 sts, turn. 27 sts.
Row 17: Ch 1, HDC in next 12 sts, HDC3tog, HDC in next 12 sts, turn. 25 sts.
Row 18: Ch 1, HDC in next 11 sts, HDC3tog, HDC in next 11 sts, turn. 23 sts.
Row 19: Ch 1, HDC in next 10 sts, HDC3tog, HDC in next 10 sts, turn. 21 sts.
Row 20: Ch 1, HDC in next 9 sts, HDC3tog, HDC in next 9 sts, turn. 19 sts.
Row 21: Ch 1, HDC in next 8 sts, HDC3tog, HDC in next 8 sts, turn. 17 sts.
Row 22: Ch 1, HDC in next 7 sts, HDC3tog, HDC in next 7 sts, turn. 15 sts.
Row 23: Ch 1, HDC in next 6 sts, HDC3tog, HDC in next 6 sts, turn. 13 sts.
Row 24: Ch 1, HDC in next 5 sts, HDC3tog, HDC in next 5 sts, turn. 11 sts.
Row 25: Ch 1, HDC in next 4 sts, HDC3tog, HDC in next 4 sts, turn. 9 sts.
Row 26: Ch 1, HDC in next 3 sts, HDC3tog, HDC in next 3 sts, turn. 7 sts.
Row 27: Ch 1, HDC in next 2 sts, HDC3tog, HDC in next 2 sts, turn. 5 sts.
Row 28: Ch 1, HDC in next 1 sts, HDC3tog, HDC in next 1 sts, turn. 3 sts.
Row 29: Ch 1, HDC3tog. Do not turn. 1 st.

Edging
Ch 1, HDC in first st and each along each side, working 3 HDC in each corner, all the way to beg, 2 HDC in corner, ch 11, sl st in top of next st to join.
Fasten off.

Finishing
Weave in ends, wash, and block to size.

Jazz Age

by Jenny Catchings | 55547

Even flappers and philosophers have to do the wash, right? With a 4-row repeat of alternating fan and V-stitches, this little cloth is complicated-looking but surprisingly easy to memorize. Crocheted in a cotton-linen blend, so you can use as a facecloth (and all that jazz).

FINISHED MEASUREMENTS
10" square

YARN
CotLin™ (DK weight, 70% Tanguis Cotton, 30% Linen, 123 yards/50g): Whisker 24834, 1 skein

HOOKS
US G/6 (4mm) Crochet hook or size needed to obtain gauge

NOTIONS
Yarn Needle
Scissors

GAUGE
4 shells = 4" in pattern stitch, unblocked

Special Stitches
V-Stitch (V-St)
1 DC, ch 1, 1 DC in 1 st

DIRECTIONS
Ch 42.
Row 1: SC in second ch from hook, *sk 3 ch, 9 DC into next ch, sk 3 ch, SC into next ch; rep from * until end, turn.
Row 2: Ch 3, 1 DC into first st, *ch 5, sk 9 DC group, work V-St [1 DC, ch 1, 1 DC] into next SC; rep from *, ending with ch 5, sk last 9 DC group, 2 DC into last SC, turn.
Row 3: Ch 3, 4 DC into first st, *(working over next ch-5 sp so as to enclose it) 1 SC into fifth DC of 9 DC group in row below, 9 DC into ch 1 of V-St; rep from *, ending with 1 SC into fifth DC from 9 DC group in row below, 5 DC into top of Tch, turn.
Row 4: Ch 3, sk 5 DC group, V-St into next SC, *ch 5, sk 9 DC group, V-St into next SC; rep from *, ending with V-St into last SC, ch 2, sl st into top of Tch, turn.
Row 5: Ch 1, 1 SC over sl st into first st of row below, *9 DC into ch-1 next V-St, (working over next ch 5 so as to enclose it) 1 SC into fifth DC from 9 DC group in row below; rep from *, ending with 1 SC into fifth DC last 9 DC group, 9 DC into ch-1 sp of next V-St, 1 SC into first ch of Tch, turn.

Rows 6–25: Rep Rows 2-5 five more times.
Row 26: Ch 3, 1 DC into first st, *ch 3, 1 SC into fifth DC of 9 DC group, ch 3, V-St into next SC; rep from * until end. Join to work in the rnd.

Border
Rnd 1: Ch 1, turn to work 1 SC in each sp along the outer perimeter of the dishcloth, with 2 SC in each corner sp; complete rnd with sl st into starting SC.
Rnd 2: Ch 1, work 1 SC into each st; complete rnd with sl st into starting SC, cut yarn and fasten off.

Finishing
Weave in ends, wash, and block to size.

Rib Texture

by Tian Connaughton | 56038

Take your crochet skills to the next level. This dishcloth uses front and back post stitches to create this rib texture and once finished, you'll have a useful piece for your kitchen.

FINISHED MEASUREMENTS
8.25" square

YARN
Dishie™ (worsted weight, 100% Cotton, 190 yards/100g): Clementine 25403, 1 skein

HOOKS
US H/8 (5mm) Crochet hook or size needed to obtain gauge

NOTIONS
Yarn Needle
Scissors

GAUGE
8 sts = 2.5" and 2 rows = 0.75" in pattern

DIRECTIONS
Ch 30.
Row 1: Sk first 2 ch, HDC in each ch across, turn. 28 sts.
Row 2: Ch 2, (HDC in Blp in next 4 sts, FPDC around next 4 sts) 3 times, HDC in Blp in last 4 sts, turn.
Row 3: Ch 2, (HDC in Flp in next 4 sts, BPDC around next 4 sts) 3 times, HDC in Flp in last 4 sts, turn.

Rep Rows 2-3 until piece measure 8.25" long.
Fasten off.

Finishing
Weave in ends, wash, and block to size.

Sloped Lines
by Jenny Konopinski | 55553

The Sloped Lines dishcloth takes the simple double crochet and adds a bit of a twist! By working a spiked crochet stitch into a previous double crochet, an interesting zigzag pattern begins to unfold—revealing lines that weave around the clusters of double crochets.

FINISHED MEASUREMENTS
7.5" square

YARN
CotLin™ (DK weight, 70% Tanguis Cotton, 30% Linen, 123 yards/50g): Sagebrush 25777, 1 skein

HOOKS
US G/6 (4mm) Crochet hook or size needed to obtain gauge

NOTIONS
Yarn Needle
Scissors

GAUGE
4.5 sts = 1" in stitch pattern

Special Stitches
Spiked Crochet
YO, insert hook into same st that the first DC of previous 3 DC section was worked, YO, draw up lp loosely as to not crush 3 DC section, *YO, draw through 2 lps* twice.

DIRECTIONS
Ch 36.
Row 1: DC in third ch from hook (counts as DC throughout), *DC into next 3 ch, Spiked Crochet in next, sk next ch* rep to end of row, work DC into last ch, turn.
Row 2: Ch 3, sk 1, * DC into next 3 sts, Spiked Crochet in next, sk next st * rep to end of row, DC into Tch, turn.

Rep Row 2 until dishcloth measures 7.5" long.

Finishing
Weave in ends, wash, and block to size.

Sherbet Tunisian

by Heidi Wells | 55574

If you want to practice your Tunisian crochet skills, dishcloths are a great project—quick and useful! This pattern features colorful stripes, just like sweet yummy sherbet.

FINISHED MEASUREMENTS
6" square

YARN
Dishie™ (worsted weight, 100% Cotton, 190 yards/100g): C1 Blush 26668, C2 Conch 25411, C3 Clementine 25403, 1 skein each

HOOKS
US H/8 (5mm) Crochet hook or size needed to obtain gauge

NOTIONS
Yarn Needle
Scissors

GAUGE
20 sts and 18 rows = 4"

Notes
Keep in mind that you will work back and forth and never turn. The right side of your work is always facing you. For the Forward Row, you will insert the hook through vertical bars created by the previous row.

There will be a Forward Row and a Return Row. On the Forward Row, you will be working right to left, and on the Return Row, you will work left to right. Basically, you are just zig-zagging back and forth. Try to work loosely if possible. This will help prevent your work from curling. Tunisian crochet fabric does tend to curl a bit, but that is easily fixed with some blocking!

When two stitches remain at the end of the Return Row, use the new color to draw through both loops. Work the forward row as usual.

DIRECTIONS
With C1, ch 30.
Preparation Row: Working into the bumps of the back side of the ch, start with the second bump from the hook, insert the hook into the bump, YO and pull a lp through, leaving it on the hook, rep until end of foundation ch.
Row 2 (Return Row): Ch 1, YO pull a lp through the next two sts on the hook, rep until one st rem on the hook.
Row 3 (Forward Row): Sk first vertical bar, insert hook into the second vertical bar, YO pull lp through, leaving it on the hook (two lps on hook), rep across.

Rep Rows 2-3 for 1.5" or desired size, ending with Row 2.
With C2, rep Row 3, then Rows 2-3 for 1", ending with Row 2.
With C3, rep Row 3, then Rows 2-3 for 1.5".
With C2, rep Row 3, then Rows 2-3 for 1", ending with Row 2.
With C1, rep Row 3, then Rows 2-3 for 1.5", ending after Row 2.

Finishing
Finish on a Forward Row. Insert the hook into the first vertical strand, yo draw lp through both vertical strand and st on hook. Rep this step of drawing a lp through both vertical st and st on the hook until the end of the row. Fasten off, pull through last lp.

Weave in ends, wash, and block to size.

Fruity Loops

by Heidi Wells | 55582

Start your day off right with a dishcloth of deliciously intense fruit flavors. The star stitch is not only fun and relatively simple, but also crochets along very quickly. It creates a wonderfully textured stitch and thick, sturdy fabric.

FINISHED MEASUREMENTS
5.5" square

YARN
Dishie™ (worsted weight, 100% Cotton, 190 yards/100g): C1 Fiesta Red 25786, C2 Begonia 25790, C3 Clementine 25403, C4 Crème Brulee 25404, C5 Honeydew 25410, C6 Azure 25412, C7 Mulberry 25784, 1 skein each

HOOKS
US I/9 (5.5mm) Crochet hook or size needed to obtain gauge

NOTIONS
Yarn Needle
Scissors

GAUGE
5 Star Stitches = 5.5" (approximately 21 sts)

Special Stitches

Star Stitch Foundation Row
Start with an odd number of chs.
1. Pull up a lp in second ch from hook and next 4 sts (6 lps on hook).
2. YO, pull through all 6 lps on hook (first Star Stitch).
3. Ch 1 to close the star (referred to as "eye" of star).
4. Insert hook into eye of previously completed star, pull up lp (2 lps on hook).
5. Insert hook into back leg of last lp of previous star, pull up a lp (3 lps on hook).
6. Insert hook into same ch as you worked the last lp of previous star, pull up a lp (4 lps on hook).
7. Pull up a lp in the next two sts (6 lps on hook).
8. YO, pull through all 6 lps, ch 1 to close star (second star created).
9. Rep steps 4-8 across row to last st, HDC in last st.

DIRECTIONS
Ch 21.

Row 1: With C1 HDC in first st, work Star Stitch Foundation Row across to last ch, HDC, turn.
Row 2: Ch 1, SC in first st, SC in "eye" of the next star, 2 SC in the eye of each Star Stitch across to last st, SC in the top of Tch, turn.
Row 3: With C2 ch 2, YO, insert hook in second ch from hook, pull up a lp, pull up a lp in next 4 sts, YO, pull through all 6 lps on hook, ch 1, rep steps 4-8 of Star Stitch Foundation Row across to last st, HDC in the same ch as last lp of previous star.
Row 4: Rep Row 2.
Rows 5-6: With C3, rep Rows 3 & 2.
Rows 7-8: With C4, rep Rows 3 & 2.
Rows 9-10: With C5, rep Rows 3 & 2.
Rows 11-12: With C6, rep Rows 3 & 2.
Rows 13-14: With C7, rep Rows 3 & 2. Fasten off.

Finishing
Weave in ends, wash, and block to size.

Multi Chevron

by Sara Dudek | 58088

Use basic tapestry crochet to create a fashion-forward look when you use Dishie Multi yarn. Its variegated color palettes bring a surprise element when used to create a stylish chevron pattern.

FINISHED MEASUREMENTS
9" square

YARN
Dishie™ (worsted weight, 100% Cotton; 190 yards/100g): C1 Swan 25409, 1 skein
Dishie™ Multi (worsted weight, 100% Cotton; 190 yards/100g): C2 Cup and Saucer 28093, 1 skein

HOOKS
US I/9 (5.5mm) Crochet hook or size needed to obtain gauge

NOTIONS
Yarn Needle
Scissors

GAUGE
17 sts and 17 rows = 4" over Single Crochet

Special Stitches
Color Changes
With C1, work in a SC according to the chart. Follow the color work chart until the st before changing to C2. Work the st before changing in C1, finishing the st by changing to C2 for the final YO, and pull through 2 lps. Work over the non-working color so there are no floats.

DIRECTIONS
With C1, ch 36.
Row 1 (RS): SC in second ch from hook and in each ch across, turn. 35 SC.
Row 2 (WS): Ch 1, SC in each SC across, turn.
Row 3: Ch 1 and join C2, work SC across according to color chart, working over the non-working sts, turn.
Rows 4-35: Rep Row 3 working according to the corresponding colorwork chart.
Don't fasten off.

Rotate the work 90 degrees and with C1, begin working a SC border around the perimeter of the project. Cut yarn and fasten off.

Finishing
Weave in ends, wash, and block to size.

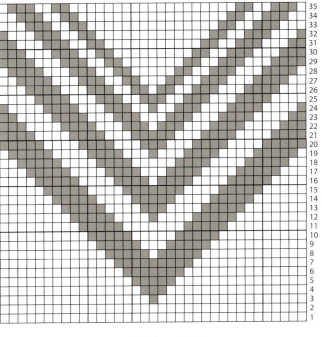

Multi Chevron Chart

Legend ☐ C1 ■ C2

Granny's Rainbow

by Beth Major | 55812

Create a colorful splash in your kitchen with a classic stitch pattern in a fun color range. Rotate the center starter color of your Granny's Rainbow dishcloth to create a matching set or use only two alternating colors to match your décor.

FINISHED MEASUREMENTS
7" square

YARN
CotLin™ (DK weight, 70% Tanguis Cotton, 30% Linen, 123 yards/50g): C1 Moroccan Red 23996, C2 Clementine 24460, C3 Canary 24837, C4 Sprout 24462, C5 Surf 24459, C6 Nightfall 23991, C7 Blackberry 24467, 1 skein each

HOOKS
US G/6 (4mm) Crochet hook or size needed to obtain gauge

NOTIONS
Yarn Needle
Scissors

GAUGE
16 sts and 8 rows = 4" over Double Crochet

DIRECTIONS
With C1, ch 5, join with sl st to form a ring.

Rnd 1: With C1, ch 3 (counts as first DC here and throughout), 2 DC in ring, ch 2, (3 DC in ring, ch 2) 3 times, join with sl st in Tch, fasten off. Do not turn.

Rnd 2: Join C2 with sl st to any ch-2 sp, ch 3, (2 DC, ch 2, 3 DC) all in same ch-2 sp, ch 1, (3 DC, ch 2, 3 DC, ch 1) in each ch-2 sp around, join with sl st in Tch, fasten off. Do not turn.

Rnd 3: Join C3 with sl st to any ch-2 sp, ch 3, (2 DC, ch 2, 3 DC) all in same ch-2 sp, ch 1, 3 DC in next ch-1 sp, ch 1, (3 DC, ch 2, 3 DC) in next ch-2 sp, ch 1, 3 DC in next ch-1 sp, ch 1* rep from * to * around, join with sl st in Tch, fasten off. Do not turn.

Rnd 4: Join C4 with sl st to any ch-2 sp, ch 3, (2 DC, ch 2, 3 DC) all in same ch-2 sp, ch 1, (3 DC in next ch-1 sp, ch 1) twice, *(3 DC, ch 2, 3 DC) in next ch-2 sp, ch 1, (3 DC in next ch-1 sp, ch 1) twice * rep from * to * around, join with sl st in Tch, fasten off. Do not turn.

Rnd 5: Join C5 with sl st to any ch-2 sp, ch 3, (2 DC, ch 2, 3 DC) all in same ch-2 sp, ch 1, (3 DC in next ch-1 sp, ch 1) three times, *(3 DC, ch 2, 3 DC) in next ch-2 sp, ch 1, (3 DC in next ch-1 sp, ch 1) three times* rep from * to * around, join with sl st in Tch, fasten off. Do not turn.

Rnd 6: Join C6 with sl st to any ch-2 sp, ch 3, (2 DC, ch 2, 3 DC) all in same ch-2 sp, ch 1, (3 DC in next ch-1 sp, ch 1) four times, *(3 DC, ch 2, 3 DC) in next ch-2 sp, ch 1, (3 DC in next ch-1 sp, ch 1) four times * rep from * to * around, join with sl st in Tch, fasten off. Do not turn.

Rnd 7: Join C7 with sl st to any ch-2 sp, ch 3, (2 DC, ch 2, 3 DC) all in same ch-2 sp, ch 1, (3 DC in next ch-1 sp, ch 1) five times, *(3 DC, ch 2, 3 DC) in next ch-2 sp, ch 1, (3 DC in next ch-1 sp, ch 1) five times * rep from * to * around, join with sl st in Tch, fasten off. Do not turn.

Finishing
Weave in ends, wash, and block to size.

Diagonal Cloth

by Beth Major | 55803

This dishcloth is designed to aid the beginner crocheter to learn the concepts of increasing and decreasing along the edge of a project and changing yarn colors within a project.

FINISHED MEASUREMENTS
8" square

YARN
CotLin™ (DK, 70% Tanguis Cotton, 30% Linen, 123 yards/50g): MC Wallaby 25775, C1 Lichen 26674, 1 skein each

HOOKS
US H/8 (5mm) Crochet hook or size needed to obtain gauge

NOTIONS
Yarn Needle
Scissors

GAUGE
12 sts = 4" in Double Crochet

Special Stitches
Double Crochet 2 Together (DC2tog)
YO, insert hook in first st, YO, pull up a lp, YO, pull through 2 lps (2 lps on hook), YO, insert hook in next st, YO, pull up a lp, YO, pull through 2 lps (3 lps on hook), YO, pull through all 3 lps.

DIRECTIONS
Row 1: With MC, ch 5, 2 DC in fourth ch from hook, 2 DC in last ch. 4 sts.
Row 2: Ch 3, turn, DC in same DC (first DC), DC in each DC across, 2 DC in turning ch.
Row 3 (and every odd row): Change color, carry unused color along side of work, rep Row 2.
Row 4 (and every even row): Rep Row 2.
Rows 5-12: Continue rep Rows 3-4. 27 sts.
Row 13: Change color, carry unused color along side of work. Ch 3, turn, DC2tog, DC in each DC across to last 2 sts, DC2tog over the last DC and the turning ch.
Row 14: Ch 3, turn, DC2tog, DC in each DC across to last 2 sts, DC2tog over the last DC and the turning ch.
Row 15 (and every odd row): Rep Row 13.
Row 16 (and every even row): Rep Row 14.
Rows 17-24: Continue rep Rows 13-14. 5 sts.
Fasten off.

Finishing
Attach MC with sl st edging color into center st of last 5 sts in last row (should be third st from either edge), ch 1, 3 SC in same st, *evenly sp 25 SC along side of work, 3 SC in next corner, rep from * 2 times, 25 SC evenly along the last edge, join with sl st to first SC. Fasten off.

Weave in ends, wash, and block to size.

Picnic Basket

by Kim Cameron | 55567

The Picnic Basket dishcloth has great texture by using alternating front post and back post double crochet, giving the look of a woven basket. This pattern, with a change in yarn, can be easily expanded to create a scarf or blanket with great drape.

FINISHED MEASUREMENTS
9" square

YARN
Dishie™ (worsted weight, 100% Cotton, 190 yards/100g): Honeydew 25410, 1 skein

HOOKS
US G/6 (4.25mm) Crochet hook or size needed to obtain gauge

NOTIONS
Yarn Needle
Scissors

GAUGE
16 sts and 10 rows = 4" over Double Crochet, blocked

Special Stitches

Front Post Double Crochet (FPDC)
YO, insert hook into gap between two sts from front to back, then around the post and out to the front side of the work. Wrap yarn around hook and draw a lp onto hook (pulling the hook back out the way you went in) 3 lps on hook. Now make the DC in the normal manner (YO, draw through 2 lps, you draw through rem 2 lps on the hook).

Back Post Double Crochet (BPDC)
YO, insert hook into gap between two sts from back to front, then around the post and out to the back side of the work. Wrap yarn around hook and draw a lp onto hook (pulling the hook back out the way you went in). 3 lps on hook. Now make the DC in the normal manner (YO, draw through 2 lps, you draw through rem 2 lps on the hook).

DIRECTIONS
Ch 38.
Row 1: DC in fourth ch from hook, DC across, turn.
Row 2 (WS): Ch 2, HDC in first 2 sts, *FP next 4 sts, BP next 4 sts, rep from * finishing with HDC in next st, HDC into top of Tch, turn.
Rows 3-4: Rep Row 2.
Row 5: Ch 2, HDC in first 2 sts, *BP next 4 sts, FP next 4 sts, rep from * finishing with HDC, HDC in next st, HDC into top of Tch, turn.
Rows 6-7: Rep Row 5.
Rep Rows 2–7 three more times.
Rep Rows 2–4 once.
Last Row: SC across.

Finishing
Weave in ends, wash, and block to size.

Picnic Basket Stitch Chart

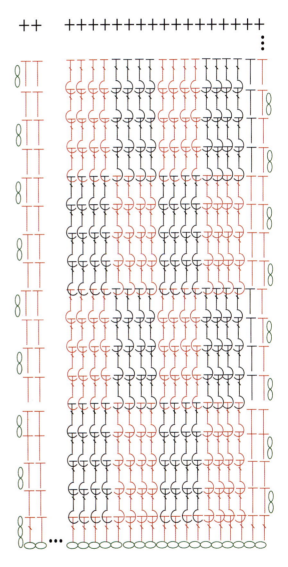

Legend

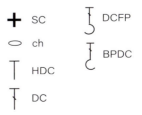

Snuggle Stitch

by Heather Mann | 58326

Create a textured dishcloth with lots of room for color play. This special stitch makes for a super-absorbent cloth that will become your go-to for dishcloths that make great housewarming gifts.

FINISHED MEASUREMENTS
9" square

YARN
Dishie™ (worsted weight, 100% Cotton, 190 yards/100g): MC Swan 25409, C1 Blush 26668, C3 Conch 25411, C4 Clementine 25403, C5 Crème Brulee 25404, C6 Honeydew 25410, C7 Verdigris 28098, C8 Kenai 25788, C9 Clarity 27037, 1 skein each

Dishie™ Twist (worsted weight, 100% Cotton, 190 yards/100g): C2 Conch 28247, 1 skein

HOOKS
US 7 (4.75mm) Crochet hook or size needed to obtain gauge

NOTIONS
Yarn Needle
Scissors

GAUGE
18 sts and 16 rows = 4" over stitch pattern, blocked

Special Stitches

Snuggle Stitch Pattern
Row 1: *DC in next 2 sts, ch 2, sk 2 st; rep across, turn.
Row 2: Working over ch, DC in DC from previous row, ch 2, sk 2 sts; rep across, turn.

DIRECTIONS
With C1, ch 39.
Row 1: With C1, ch 2, DC in 1 st, ch 2, sk 2 sts, *DC in next 2 sts, ch 2, sk 2 sts; rep from * across, turn.
Row 2: With C2, ch 2, working over ch, DC in DC from previous row, ch 2, sk 2 sts, *DC in next 2 sts, ch 2, sk 2 sts; rep from * across, turn.
Row 3: Rep Row 2.
Rows 4-5: With C3, rep Row 2.
Rows 6-7: With C4, rep Row 2.
Rows 8-9: With C5, rep Row 2.
Rows 10-11: With C6, rep Row 2.
Rows 12-13: With C7, rep Row 2.
Rows 14-15: With C8, rep Row 2.
Rows 16-17: With C9, rep Row 2.
Rows 18-30: With MC, rep Row 2.

Finishing
Weave in ends, wash, and block to size.

Snuggle Stitch Chart

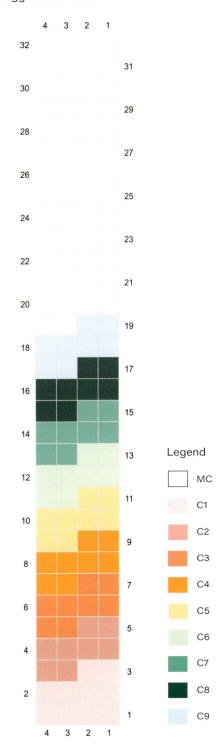

Gingham Twist

by Sara Dudek | 58087

Dishie Twist combines white and color in a steady twist, making it perfect for creating a playful gingham pattern. This simple tapestry crochet dishcloth is sure to dress up your kitchen!

FINISHED MEASUREMENTS
9" square

YARN
Dishie™ (worsted weight, 100% Cotton; 190 yards/100g): C1 Blue 25787, C2 Swan 25409, 1 skein each

Dishie™ Twist (worsted weight, 100% Cotton; 190 yards/100g): C3 Blue 28244, 1 skein

HOOKS
US I/9 (5.5mm) Crochet hook or size needed to obtain gauge

NOTIONS
Yarn Needle
Scissors

GAUGE
17 sts and 17 rows = 4" over Single Crochet

Notes
Use simple single crochet stitches worked in rows with tapestry crochet color changes every 4 stitches. Simply work back and forth in rows, changing colors regularly to create the color blocks, then work a single crochet border around the edge.

Special Stitches

Color Changes
Work in a SC in the old color until the st before changing to the new color. With working color, insert hook in st, YO, pull up a lp, with new color YO and pull through 2 lps on hook. Work over the non-working color so there are no floats.

DIRECTIONS
With C1, ch 41.
Row 1 (RS): With C1, ch 1, *with C1, SC in next 4 sts, change to C3 and work SC in each of the next 4 sts, rep from * across, turn.
Row 2 (WS): With C3, ch 1, *with C3, SC in next 4 sts, change to C1 and work SC in each of next 4 sts, rep from * across, turn.
Rows 3-4: Rep Rows 1-2.
Row 5: With C3, ch 1, *with C3 SC in next 4 sts, change to C2 and work SC in each of next 4 sts, rep from * across, turn.
Row 6: With C2, ch 1, *with C2 SC in next 4 sts, change to C3 and work SC in each of next 4 sts, rep from * across, turn.
Rows 7-8: Rep Rows 5-6. Rep Rows 1-8, 4 more times. With C1 rotate the work 90 degrees and with C1, begin working a SC border around the perimeter of the project. Fasten off.

Finishing
Weave in ends, wash, and block to size.

Brick-a-Brack

by Beth Major | 55855

Learn how to manage your crochet tension by creating a beautiful set of cloths to match your kitchen décor.

FINISHED MEASUREMENTS
10" square

YARN
Shine™ (sport weight, 60% Pima Cotton, 40% Modal® natural beech wood fiber, 110 yards/50g): MC Sweet Potato 26675, C1 Serenade 24487, 1 skein each

HOOKS
US G/6 (4mm) Crochet hook or size needed to obtain gauge

NOTIONS
Yarn Needle
Scissors

GAUGE
16 sts and 20 rows = 4" over Single Crochet

Special Stitches

Deep V-SC
Insert hook into designated ch 1 sp, YO and pull up a lp even with your stitching (be careful to do this fairly loosely, too much tension with cause the sts to pull up and squeeze together) YO and pull though both lps.

DIRECTIONS
With C1, ch 44.

Row 1: Row 1: SC in second ch from hook , SC across, turn. 43 sts.

Row 2: With MC ch 1, SC in next 6 SC, *ch 1, sk 1, SC in next 5 SC* rep from * to * across, SC in last SC, turn.

Row 3: Ch 2, HDC in each SC and ch-1 sp across, turn.

Row 4: Ch 1, SC across, turn.

Row 5: With C1, ch 1, SC in first SC, *SC in next 5 SC, work Deep V-SC in ch-1 sp from Row 2, sk SC under the Deep V-SC, * rep from * to * across, SC in last 6 SC, turn.

Row 6: With MC, ch 1, SC in first 3 SC, *ch 1, sk next SC, SC in next 5 SC* rep from * to * across, SC in last 3 SC, turn.

Row 7: Rep Row 3.

Row 8: Rep Row 4.

Row 9: With C1, ch 1, SC in first 3 SC, work Deep V-SC into ch-1 sp from Row 6, sk SC under deep V-SC, *SC in next 5 SC, work Deep V-SC into ch-1 sp from Row 6, sk SC under deep V-SC * rep from * to * across, SC in last 3 SC.

Rep Rows 2-9 until cloth measures approximately 10" long ending with a Row 5 or a Row 9, do not fasten off, and do not turn.

Edging
With C1, *3 SC in corner, work 43 SC along edge of cloth* rep 3 more times, join with sl st. Fasten off.

Finishing
Weave in ends, wash, and block to size.

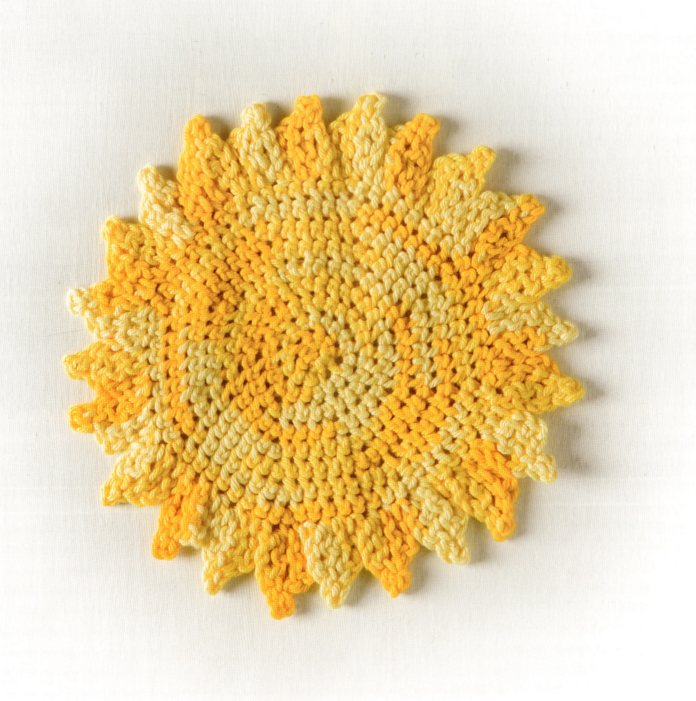

The Sun's Out!

by Jennifer Pionk | 56003

Keep your kitchen in permanent sunshine with this sweet dishcloth! The center of the sun is worked in continuous rounds to keep from having an unsightly seam. Lastly, the flames are added for a final touch!

FINISHED MEASUREMENTS
7.5" diameter

YARN
Dishie™ Multi (worsted weight, 100% Cotton, 190 yards/100g): Sunshine 27341, 1 skein

HOOKS
US H/8 (5mm) Crochet hook or size needed to obtain gauge

NOTIONS
Yarn Needle
Stitch Marker
Scissors

GAUGE
2.5" diameter after Rnd 4

DIRECTIONS

Center of Sun
Work in continuous rnds beginning at the end of Rnd 1. PM after the last st of the current rnd before moving on to the next rnd. Move the marker up to the current rnd as you work.

Work this entire section in back loops only.

Rnd 1: Begin with a Magic Circle, ch 1, work 8 SC into Magic Circle. 8 sts.
Rnd 2: 2 SC in each st around. 16 sts.
Rnd 3: *2 SC in the next st, SC in the next st, rep from * around. 24 sts.
Rnd 4: *2 SC in the next st, SC in each of the next 2 sts, rep from * around. 32 sts.
Rnd 5: *2 SC in the next st, SC in each of the next 3 sts, rep from * around. 40 sts.
Rnd 6: *2 SC in the next st, SC in each of the next 4 sts, rep from * around. 48 sts.
Rnd 7: *2 SC in the next st, SC in each of the next 5 sts, rep from * around. 56 sts.
Rnd 8: *2 SC in the next st, SC in each of the next 6 sts, rep from * around. 64 sts.
Rnd 9: *2 SC in the next st, SC in each of the next 7 sts, rep from * around. 72 sts.

Flames
Work this entire round in back loops only.
Rnd 1: *Ch 3, tr in the next st, ch 3, sl st in the third ch from your hook, tr in the next st, ch 2, sl st in the same st as the tr you just worked**, sl st in the next st, rep from * around, ending last rep at **. 24 flames.

Finishing
Weave in ends, wash, and block to size.

Marguerite

by Heidi Wells | 55592

This striking dishcloth combines rounded peaks and pretty points to create a dazzling, fan-like effect. The color combinations for this pattern are endless.

FINISHED MEASUREMENTS
9.5" wide x 8.5" high

YARN
Comfy™ (worsted weight, 75% Pima Cotton, 25% Acrylic, 109 yards/50g): C1 Rosehip 25769, C2 White 25315, C3 Silver Sage 24424, C4 Whisker 24800, 1 skein each

HOOKS
US J/10 (6mm) Crochet hook or size needed to obtain gauge

NOTIONS
Yarn Needle
Scissors

GAUGE
1 shell = 2"

Special Stitches

Clamshell Spike Stitch
(Over 3 sl sts)
Sk first sl st, 1 DC into SC under second sl st, 1 DC into the SC of the row below that (3 rows down), 1 DC into SC under second sl st again, sk third sl st.

DIRECTIONS
With C1, ch 34.

Setup Row
Row 1: SC in second ch from hook, SC across, turn.
Row 2: Ch 1, SC across, turn.

Pattern Repeat
Row 3: Sl st in next 2 st, *HDC in next st, DC in next 3, HDC in next st, sl st in next 3 sts* rep from * to * to last 2 sts, sl st in last 2 sts, turn.
Row 4: With C2, ch 3 (counts as DC), DC in next sl st, *HDC into HDC, SC in next 3 DC, HDC in HDC, work Clamshell Spike Stitch*, rep from * to * to last 2 sl sts, SC in each sl sts, turn.
Row 5: Ch 1, SC across, turn.
Row 6: Ch 3 (counts as DC), DC in next st, *HDC, sl st over next 3 st, HDC, DC in next 3 st* rep from * to * to last 2 sts, DC in last 2 sts, turn.
Row 7: With C3, ch 1, SC in same st, SC in next st *HDC in HDC, work Clamshell Spike Stitch, HDC in HDC, SC in next 3 DC* rep from * to * to last 2 sts, SC in last 2 sts, turn.
Row 8: Ch 1, SC across, turn.
Row 9: Rep Row 3.
Rows 10-12: With C4, rep Rows 4-6.
Rows 13-15: With C1, rep Rows 7-9.

Rep Rows 4-15 once more, changing colors where indicated.

Rep Rows 4-5 once more, fasten off.

Finishing
Weave in ends, wash, and block to size.

C2C Color Fade

by Sarah Nairalez | 58325

This dishcloth is simple and a great first Corner to Corner (C2C) project. With basic color changes, this dishcloth will add a pop of color to your kitchen. There's a practical loop on one corner, making it easy to hang. In the Corner to Corner (C2C) technique, each block is made of a 3 chains and 3 double crochet and the project is worked from one corner to the other.

FINISHED MEASUREMENTS
10" square

YARN
Shine™ (sport weight, 60% Pima Cotton, 40% Modal® natural beech wood fiber, 110 yards/50g): C1 Sailor 25336, C2 French Blue 24783, C3 Sky 23621, 1 skein each

HOOKS
US E/4 (3.5mm) Crochet hook or size needed to obtain gauge

NOTIONS
Yarn Needle
Scissors

GAUGE
6.5 blocks and 6.5 rows = 4"

DIRECTIONS
With C1, ch 6.
Row 1 (RS): DC in fourth ch from hook (sk first 3 ch count as ch-3 sp here and throughout), DC in next 2 ch, turn. 1 block.
Row 2 (WS): Ch 6, DC in fourth ch from hook, DC in next 2 ch, (sl st, ch 3, 3 DC) in next ch-3 sp, turn. 2 blocks.
Row 3: Ch 6, DC in fourth ch from hook, DC in next 2 ch, *(sl st, ch 3, 3 DC) in next ch-3 sp; rep from * across, turn. 3 blocks.
Row 4: Ch 6, DC in fourth ch from hook, DC in next 2 ch, *(sl st, ch 3, 3 DC) in next ch-3 sp; rep from * across, turn. 4 blocks.
Rows 5-10: With C2, rep Row 4, finishing Row 10 with 10 blocks.
Rows 11-15: With C3, rep Row 4, finishing Row 15 with 15 blocks.
Row 16: Ch 1, sl st in next 3 DC, sl st in Tch, continue creating blocks acorss the new row, ending with a sl st in the ch 4 turning ch, turn.
Rows 17-20: With C3, rep Row 16, finishing Row 20 with 11 blocks.
Rows 21-26: With C2, rep Row 16, finishing Row 26 with 5 blocks.
Rows 27-30: With C1, rep Row 16, finishing Row 30 with one block, do not fasten off where you started. Don't cut the yarn.

Hanging Loop
Row 1: With C1, ch 30, sl st in the starting ch.
Row 2: Ch 1, SC around the lp. 30 sts.

Cut yarn, leaving a tail twice as long as dishcloth. Wrap the long tall around the base of the lp to the desired look. Use a crochet hook to bring the end of the yarn up and throw the wrapped yarn. Tie to fasten off.

Finishing
Weave in ends, wash, and block to size.

C2C Color Fade Chart

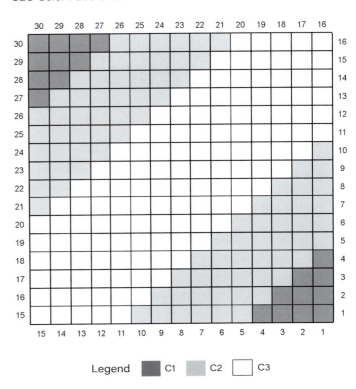

Legend: C1 C2 C3

Custard Pie

by Heidi Wells | 55588

This easy shell stitch center creates a delectable, textured effect, snugly framed by a chunky single crochet border.

FINISHED MEASUREMENTS
8.25" square

YARN
Dishie™ (worsted weight, 100% Cotton, 190 yards/100g): Crème Brulee 25404, 1 skein

HOOKS
US J/10 (6mm) Crochet hook or size needed to obtain gauge

NOTIONS
Yarn Needle
Scissors

GAUGE
4 shells = 4"

DIRECTIONS
Ch 22 (or a multiple of 3 + 1).
Row 1: DC in fourth ch from hook, sk 3 sts, SC in fourth st, *ch 3, 3 DC in same st as SC, sk 3 sts, SC in the next st, rep from * to last 2 sts, SC in the last st, turn.
Row 2: Ch 3, 3 DC same st, *[SC, ch 3, 3 DC] in next ch-3 sp, rep from * across to last st, SC in last ch-3 sp, turn.

Rep Row 2 seven times or until you reach the desired size.

Last Row: Ch 2, 3 DC in same st, *SC in the next ch-3 sp, 3 DC in the sp connecting the ch 3 just worked into and previous cluster of DC sts, continue from * across.

Edging
Turn, ch 1, SC evenly around the border, making sure to work 2 SC in each corner.
Rep for 3 rows or until desired size of border, fasten off.

Finishing
Weave in ends, wash, and block to size.

A Chance of Rain

by Hannah Maier | 55571

Rows of single crochet make this a simple, quick cloth to crochet while the added cloud and sprinkle of raindrops make it cute enough for any kitchen!

FINISHED MEASUREMENTS
9" square

YARN
Dishie™ (worsted weight, 100% Cotton, 190 yards/100g): MC Silver 25789, C1 Swan 25409, 1 skein each

CotLin™ (DK weight, 70% Tanguis Cotton, 30% Linen, 123 yards/50g): C2 Hydrangea 25772, 1 skein

HOOKS
US H/8 (5mm) Crochet hook or size needed to obtain gauge

NOTIONS
Yarn Needle
Scissors

GAUGE
15 SC and 10 rows = 4"

DIRECTIONS

Body
With MC, ch 35.
Row 1: SC in second ch from hook, SC across, turn. 34 sts.
Row 2: Ch 1, SC across.

Rep Row 2 until cloth measures 9" long. Fasten off, weave in ends.

Cloud (make one)
With C1, ch 16.
Rnd 1: SC in second ch from hook and in each of next 13 ch, 3 SC in last ch, rotate so that the unworked side of the ch is facing up, work 14 SC across unworked side of the ch, 3 SC in Tch.
Rnd 2: SC in each st around.
Rnd 3: Sl next two sts, (1 SC, 1 HDC, 1 DC, 1 tr), (1 tr, 1 DC, 1 HDC), sl st, (1 SC, 1 HDC), 3 DC, 2 tr, 3 DC, 2 HDC, sl st, (1 SC, 1 HDC, 1 DC, 1 tr), (1 tr, 1 DC), SC in next two sts, sl st into next two sts. Fasten off, leaving a 12" long tail.

Raindrops (make three)
With C2, ch 2.
Row 1: 2 DC in second ch from hook, fasten off leaving an 8" long tail.

Finishing
Weave in all beginning tails on the cloud and raindrops. Use the long end tails to sew the cloud and drops to the dishcloth. To sew the cloud and drops to the dishcloth, whip stitch around the shapes making sure to catch only the front bar of the SC sts on the dishcloth so that your thread doesn't show on the other side of the fabric.

Legend
 tr
 DC
 ch
▶ start point
● sl st

Cloud Chart

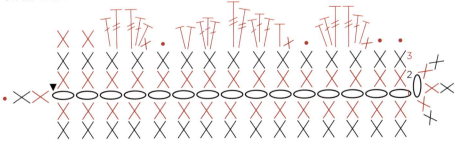

Raindrop Chart

Chevron

by Tian Connaughton | 55035

This dishcloth is created using chunky chevrons with a simple single crochet edge and loop for hanging. It works great for both multi and solid yarns.

FINISHED MEASUREMENTS
8" wide x 8.25" high

YARN
Dishie™ Multi (worsted weight, 100% Cotton, 190 yards/100g): Cup and Saucer 28093, 1 skein

HOOKS
US H/8 (5mm) Crochet hook or size needed to obtain gauge

NOTIONS
Yarn Needle
Scissors

GAUGE
12 sts = 4" and 8 rows = 3" in pattern

Special Stitches
Cluster Stitch (CL)
YO, insert hook into st indicated, pull up a lp, YO, insert into same st, pull up a lp (5 lps on hook), YO, draw through all 5 lps.

DIRECTIONS
Ch 25.
Row 1: SC in second ch from hook and in each ch across, turn. 24 sts.
Row 2: Ch 1, SC in each st across row, turn.
Row 3: Ch 1, *(SC in next SC) 4 times, (CL in next SC) 4 times; rep from * across row, turn.
Row 4: Ch 1, *(SC in next CL st) 4 times, (CL in next SC) 4 times; rep from * across row, turn.
Rep Row 4 until cloth measures 8" long, do not fasten off.

Last Row: Ch 1, SC in each st across to last st, ch 10, sl st in base of last st worked.
Fasten off.

Finishing
Weave in ends, wash, and block to size.

Sophia Spa
by Jenny Konopinski | 55566

Simple yet sophisticated, this spa cloth works up quickly with just a few stitches that are repeated row after row. The combination of repetition and simple stitches make this a great pattern for beginning crocheters looking to expand their skills.

FINISHED MEASUREMENTS
12" square

YARN
Shine™ (sport weight, 60% Pima Cotton, 40% Modal® natural beech wood fiber, 110 yards/50g): Wisteria 25333, 1 skein

HOOKS
US F/5 (3.75mm) Crochet hook or size needed to obtain gauge

NOTIONS
Yarn Needle
Scissors

GAUGE
7 half double "V stitches" = 4", blocked

DIRECTIONS
Loosely ch 42 sts.
Row 1: (HDC, ch 1, HDC) in fourth ch from hook, *sk 1, (HDC, ch 1, HDC) in next; rep from * across until last 2 ch, sk 1, HDC in last, turn.
Row 2: Ch 2, *sk 2 sts, (HDC, ch 1, HDC) in next ch-sp, rep from * to last HDC, sk next st, HDC into Tch, turn.

Finishing
Weave in ends, wash, and block to size.

Tunisian Seed Stitch

by Tian Connaughton | 56057

Use simple Tunisian stitches to create this fun and quick dishcloth. Whether you use a solid-colored yarn or a multi, the texture shines through! Completing the look is a hanging loop, perfect for use in the kitchen.

FINISHED MEASUREMENTS
9" square

YARN
Dishie™ Multi (worsted weight, 100% Cotton, 190 yards/100g): Pebble 27336, 1 skein

HOOKS
US J/10 (6mm) Tunisian hook or size needed to obtain gauge
US G/6 (4mm) Crochet hook or size needed to obtain gauge

NOTIONS
Yarn Needle
Scissors

GAUGE
16 sts and 12 rows = 4" in pattern

Special Stitches

Tunisian Simple Stitch (TSS) [forward pass]
Sk first vertical bar, *insert hook in from right to left behind next single vertical bar, YO, draw lp through and leave on hook.

Tunisian Purl Stitch (TPS) [forward pass]
Sk first vertical bar, bring yarn to front, insert hook in next vertical bar, bring yarn to back under hook, wrap around hook from back to front, draw yarn through st (purl made).

DIRECTIONS
Ch 36.
Foundation Row (forward pass): Keeping all lps on hook, sk first ch from hook (the lp on the hook is the first ch) and draw up a lp in each ch across row, do not turn.
Foundation Row (return pass): YO, draw through first lp on hook, *YO, draw through next 2 lps; rep from * across row until 1 lp rem on hook (the lp rem on the hook always counts as the first st of the next row).
Row 1 (forward pass): Sk first st, TSS in next st, *TPS in next st, TSS in next st; rep from * across, do not turn.
Row 1 (return pass): YO, draw through 1 lp, (this ch forms the edge st), *YO, draw through 2 lps; rep from * until 1 lp rem on hook (the lp left on the hook is the first st of the next row), do not turn.
Row 2 (forward pass): Sk first st, *TPS st in next st, TSS in next st, rep from * row to 1 st before end, TSS in last st.
Row 2 (return pass): YO, draw through 1 lp, (this ch forms the edge st), *YO, draw through 2 lps; rep from * until 1 lp rem on hook (the lp left on the hook is the first st of the next row), do not turn.
Rep Rows 1-2 until cloth measure 9" long.

Remove Tunisian hook from lp and replace with crochet hook. Beg working in HDC around as follow: ch 2, HDC in first st across row, 3 HDC in corner, HDC down side, 3 HDC in next corner, HDC in each foundation ch, 3 HDC in corner, HDC in edge up side to corner, ch 10, join with sl st to ch at beg of rnd.
Fasten off.

Finishing
Weave in ends, wash, and block to size.

Heirloom Linen

by Kalurah Hudson | 55847

Heirloom Linen cloth is crocheted in a pretty Linen stitch, mimicking the look of timeless linen cloth. Delicate picots and shells trim the edges of the dishcloth, lending to the vintage feel.

FINISHED MEASUREMENTS
7" wide x 22.5" high

YARN
CotLin™ (DK weight, 70% Tanguis Cotton, 30% Linen, 123 yards/50g): MC Gosling 26239, 2 skeins

Shine™ (sport weight, 60% Pima Cotton, 40% Modal® natural beech wood fiber, 110 yards/50g): C1 Cream 23615, 1 skein

HOOKS
US G/6 (4.25mm) Crochet hook or size needed to obtain gauge
US E/6 (3.5mm) Crochet hook or size needed to obtain gauge

NOTIONS
Yarn Needle
Scissors

GAUGE
11 sts and 20 rows = 4" in Linen stitch, blocked

Special Stitches

3 Double Crochet Decrease (3DCdec)
YO, insert hook into st, pull up a lp, YO and pull through 2 lps on hook, *YO, insert hook into the same st, pull up a lp, YO and pull through 2 lps on hook* 2 times, YO and pull through rem 3 st on hook.

Picot
Ch 3, sl st in first ch to close (1 picot complete).

Front Loop Single Crochet (FLSC)
Work a SC st into the front lp only.

DIRECTIONS
Body
Start with the smaller hook and MC, ch 41.
Row 1: SC in second ch from hook, SC in ea ch across, turn. 40 SC.
Switch to larger hook.
Row 2: Ch 2, sk first SC, SC in next SC, *ch 1, sk next SC, SC in next SC* rep to last sc, turn.
Row 3: Ch 2, sk first SC, SC in next ch1-sp, *ch 1, sk next SC, SC in next ch1-sp* rep to end, work last SC in the ch-2 sp, turn.
Row 4: Ch 2, sk first SC, SC in next ch-1 sp, *ch 1, sk next SC, SC in next ch-1 sp* rep to end, work last SC in the ch-2 sp, turn.
Rows 5-92: Rep Rows 3-4.
Switch to smaller hook.
Row 93: Ch 1, SC in first SC, *SC in ch-1 sp, SC in next SC* rep to end, work last SC in ch-2 sp. Fasten off.

Edging
Using smaller hook and C1, join yarn to the first SC of the cloth, with RS facing you.
Row 1: Ch 1, (does not count as first st), do not turn, SC across, turn. 40 SC.
Row 2: Ch 1, (does not count as a st), FLSC in each SC to end, turn. 40 FLSC.
Row 3: Ch 2, (does not count as a st), sk first 3 FLSC, 3DCdec into next st, picot, ch 1, 3DCdec in same st, picot, ch 1, 3DCdec in same st, * picot, ch 2, sk next 4 FLSC, SC in next FLSC, picot, SC in the next SC, ch 2, sk next 4 FLSC, 3 DCdec into next st, picot, ch 1, 3DCdec in same st, picot, ch 1, 3DCdec in same st, * rep 2 more times to fourth st from the end, picot, ch 2, sk next 2 FLSC, sl st in last FLSC. Fasten off.

Rotate dishcloth to bottom edge, with RS facing you join yarn to the first ch of foundation ch, rep Rows 1-3 of edging instructions.

Finishing
Weave in ends, wash, and block to size.